SELECTED POEMS
~
POESÍA SELECTA

SELECTED POEMS

—&— POESÍA SELECTA

Luis Palés Matos

Translated from the Spanish,
with an introduction, by Julio Marzán

Arte Público Press
Houston, Texas

This volume is made possible through grants from the Andrew W. Mellon Foundation and the City of Houston through The Cultural Arts Council of Houston, Harris County.

Esta edición ha sido subvencionada por la Fundación Andrew W. Mellon y la Ciudad de Houston por medio del Consejo Cultural de Arte de Houston, Harris County.

Recovering the past, creating the future

Recuperando el pasado, creando el futuro

Arte Público Press
University of Houston
Houston, Texas 77204-2174

Cover design by / Diseño de la portada por Giovanni Mora

Palés Matos, Luis.
    [Poems. Selections English & Spanish]
    Selected poems = poesía selecta / by Luis Palés Matos translated from the Spanish, with an introduction by, Julio Marzán.
    p. cm. — (Recovering the U.S. Hispanic literary heritage)
    ISBN 1-55885-303-0 (pbk. : alk. paper)
    1. Palés Matos, Luis-Translations into English. I. Title: Poesía selecta. II. Marzán, Julio, 1946- III. Title. IV. Recovering the U.S. Hispanic Literary Heritage Project publication.
PQ7439.P24 A26 2000
861'62-dc21
                                           00-056588
                                             CIP

∞ The paper used in this publication meets the requirements of the American National Standard for Information Sciences—Permanence of Paper for Printed Library Materials, ANSI Z39.48-1984.

Printed in the United States of America
Imprimido en los Estados Unidos

0 1 2 3 4 5 6 7 8 9   10 9 8 7 6 5 4 3 2 1

Contents

Part III (1938-1944)

Part IV (1944 -1959)

Introduction
In the Mingling Grain

Luis Palés Matos is . . . probably one of the most important
poets of all Latin America today—though many would con-
test this from a conventional viewpoint.

—*William Carlos Williams,*
from the introductory note to his translation "Prelude in Boricua"

IN 1941, WILLIAM CARLOS WILLIAMS attended the Inter-Amer-
ican Writers Conference in Puerto Rico,[1] where he met Luis Palés
Matos. This encounter with a major poet from his mother's homeland
symbolized much for Williams, who from his earliest years had set out
to identify the tributary antecedents that flowed into his cultural and
artistic genealogy, what he called—referring to both blood and poet-
ry—his "'line.'"[2] Starting with the seventeenth-century baroque poets
Góngora and Quevedo and extending to the twentieth-century Cubists
Gris and Picasso,[3] that mainly Spanish "line," his maternal legacy, also
connected him to every Spanish and Latin American writer of his time.
When traveling through Andalusia, for example, he was conscious of
the spirit of Lorca, who descended from that line. Pablo Neruda, anoth-
er spiritual brother, was portrayed in a poem by Williams as another of
his mother Elena's sons. So when in 1941 Williams and Luis Palés
Matos were introduced, Palés instantly became kindred in Williams's
reconstructed lineage.

In Palés's 1937 book *Tuntún de pasa y grifería: poesía afroanti-*
llana (Tomtom of Kinky Hair and Black Things: Afro-Caribbean

Poetry), Williams immediately recognized in its celebration of spiri-
tual and racial mingling the same ideas that he had written in his *In
the American Grain* (1925), in which he had identified "the min-
gling" as the epitome of truest American spirit, an ideal exemplified
in his mother's Caribbean. Soon after returning to Rutherford,
Williams published a translation of Palés's prefatory poem, "Preludio
en Boricua" ("Prelude in Boricua"), and used Palés as model for his
own celebration of blackness in "The Gentle Negress." (A second
version of this poem drops the Palesian touches.) Another imitation
appeared in the first book of *Paterson,* one of whose stanzas describes
the photograph of an African king on the cover of (presumably the
National) "Geographic" magazine. This stanza echoes elements of
two poems by Palés, "Elegy for the Duke of Marmalade" and "Black
Majesty."

In fact, *Paterson* itself was an adaptation of the premise of Palés's
book: a love song to a region, a poet's definition of self as informed
by a sense of place and its spiritual tributaries. Palés's organizing
metaphor was a sea; Williams's was a river. Years later, Williams
explained to the critic Edith Heal that he had been planning to write a
long poem about a man and the city but had put it off until he came
upon the "scheme" for *Paterson* "in 1941," the year in which he
attended the Puerto Rico conference.

Despite coming from sharply different geographies and national
cultures, the two poets exhibited important similarities. They both
attributed their poetic gift to a muse who was a dark beauty: Williams,
his brunette mother Elena; Palés, his fictive mulatta Filí Melé. This
muse was also their own idealized object of sexual desire, which addi-
tionally served to characterize identical poetic personae: a white man
entranced before dark beauty. Those already familiar with Palés
Matos's work know that his Afro-Caribbean poems are paeans to Anti-
Western sexual liberation and the sensuality of black women, but less
discussed among Williams's readers is his fascination with "dark
beauty" in several poems and notably in the prose piece "The Colored
Girls of Pasternack." In sum, both poets were led by dark muses
to sexually and artistically challenge a mainstream consciousness
by which they were also informed. For this reason, the work of both
poets performed a balancing act of contradictory personae: Williams,

his Bill and Carlos voices, and Palés, the white *criollo* and the spiritually-mulatto Caribbean islander.

Stylistically, both poets would appear to be polar opposites. Palés's poems patently descend from the baroque and are built around extended metaphors, underscoring wit and artifice; Williams's poetry is free verse that captures the freshness of lived, not literary, experience in spoken-sounding language. But neither poet was absolutely what he seemed. In his Afro-Caribbean poems, along with the ornate and formal structures, Palés employed a popular diction charged with the humor, irony and risqué ambiguity of the island's unprestigious, African-enriched spoken language. For his part, Williams wrote an ostensibly spontaneous language that in fact was often baroque artifice disguised as spoken directness, in his mind descending from the Spanish baroque poets Quevedo and Góngora. In the essay "Federico García Lorca," to illustrate, Williams describes Góngora as "the man," a salute that suggests that he is also the titular "El Hombre," who (in one of the several possible readings of that poem) transmits his "strange courage" to Williams.[4]

Finally, at the time they met, both poets were on parallel missions. Williams was determined to define the true American spirit (rooted in the Spanish priests and explorers, not Puritan settlers) and produce great art of American ingredients. Luis Palés Matos endeavored to define the Americanness of his Hispanic Caribbean culture and was equally determined to produce serious poetry from the devalued rhythms and images of his island's spoken language. Under the veneer of great difference, then, existed a profound kinship that Williams immediately recognized in *Tuntún*. So who was this poet whom Williams called "one of the most important" from Latin America?

∾ ∾ ∾

One of Latin America's great poets, Luis Palés Matos (1898-1959) is also one of its most controversial[5]—owing to his rhythmically rich and onomatopoetic *poesía afroantillana*, the poems that made him famous. He published a first book in 1917 as a teenager, afterwards wrote or started other manuscripts that, except for individual poems in reviews, he never published. Critics began taking him seriously around 1925 (when the selection of this book of translations begins). In that same year, he also began locally publishing his Afro-Caribbean poems, of which, in 1927 the Madrid journal *La Gaceta Literaria* re-printed a selection. For the next decade, the Afro-Caribbean poems that appeared in journals began to build Palés's reputation throughout the Spanish-speaking world, well before he collected them in 1937 under the title *Tuntún de pasa y grifería: poesía afroantillana* (Tomtom of Kinky Hair and Black Things: Afro-Caribbean Poetry).

Racially black poets existed in Spanish, of course, but in an oral or musical tradition. Palés's *poesía afroantillana,* whose first publishing in the 1920s predated the French negritude movement by a decade, introduced Afro-Caribbean rhythms, metaphors and voices to the formal Spanish-language literary consciousness. Their novelty and popularity encouraged other poets, white and black, to write what in Spanish was broadly labeled *poesía negra,* which unlike its English counterpart encompassed poems merely about black subjects, whether written by a white or black poet. For this contribution to Spanish-language poetry, despite the fact that the blond Palés was not black and his Afro-Caribbean poems comprised a phase, albeit major, of his work, he is credited with initiating *poesía negra,* and the rest of his work was literally obscured by his reputation as a *poeta negro*—even long after he explained that he wrote not of color but of a cultural and geographical consciousness that he called *afroantillana.*

This distinction failed to pacify his racially sensitive detractors in Puerto Rico, where his Afro-Caribbean poems ignited a controversy. Palés's celebrating African roots disturbed the Puerto Rican *criollo* consciousness whose cultural symbol was not the marginalized *negro* but the white *jíbaro.* Moreover, Palés was publicly Africanizing Puerto Rico at a critical time when, to defend Hispanic culture against the United States's efforts to Anglo-Americanize the island, writers and intellectuals were renewing their cultural allegiance to Mother Spain, which—about to erupt in war—itself was seen as needing its children. Eventually, even though Palés did win considerable respect at home, that respect was overshadowed by the reverence afforded the Spanish poets of the Generation of 1898, exiled in Puerto Rico from Spain's Civil War.

In time, especially owing to his later poems, critics did take note of the other facets of Palés's work but in readings that inevitably segregated the Afro-Caribbean poems. The "black" poems were read as a white man's playful satires on the black race or—the only other possible justification for his writing such poetry—as impersonal Dadaist experiments. "Black Dance" is his most anthologized and misread in this sense. His "white" poems, on the other hand, were assumed to convey his contemplative and lyrical voice. In sum, except for introducing the two kinds of poems as the output of a single biography, critics had a difficult time making unified sense of this ostensibly "black" and "white" work.

To illustrate the critics's confusion, in the 1934 *Antología de la poesía española e hispanoamericana,* Columbia professor Federico De Onís, one of Palés's earliest advocates, described *poesía afroantillana* as an innovative peak in a composite oeuvre of "white" and "black" poems. He restated that argument of a composite work in his introduction to Palés's collected poems, *Poesía 1915-1956* (1957) but never offered evidence of how the poet sustained a single discourse.

The Argentine literary historian Enrique Anderson Imbert, on the other hand, in 1959 read into *Poesía 1915-1956* a wide gulf between the "black poems," which he more or less dismissed, and the "more . . . complex and enduring [white]" poems:

> The reading of his book *Poesía 1915-1956*—published in 1957—shows a complete Palés Matos that does not remain on the surface with black themes, rather he plunges into a more profound, essential, complex and enduring poetry. Only then does one understand that those black poems . . . were . . . episodes in the expression of a sad look at elemental life and the dispersion of nothingness (see "The Call")[6]

Six years later, in a college text co-authored with the Cuban poet Eugenio Florit (*Literatura Hispanoamericana: Antología e Introducción Histórica*), Anderson Imbert contradicted that earlier assessment of the Afro-Caribbean poems by appreciating that they form a "great orchestra" playing an ironic "countersong":

In his great orchestra one hears an ironic countersong; because Palés Matos is not black, being white, and smiles before the contrasts of both cultures . . . In this ironic note, skepticism and refined melancholy . . . he is different . . . from others who work in the same genre of poetry.

This change may reflect the poet Florit's helping Anderson Imbert to read the Afro-Caribbean poems properly, but even more important, this was the first critical acknowledgment that Palés's *poesía afroantillana* was consciously a "countersong."

This shift in interpretation illustrates the difficulty that the rest of the literary world had with reading Palés, who remained two poets because his stylistic *mulatez* kept him from fitting cleanly in critical discussions of his generation of post-*modernistas.* Ocasionally, one or another critic recognized his uniqueness as an indicator of his originality. De Onís saw this nonconformity as a feature shared with other great poets:

The definition that I made of him as a post-*modernista* poet is amplified by the fact that I placed him among the ultra-*modernista* section. Palés, like López Velarde, Vallejo, Lorca or Neruda, is of the two schools simultaneously.[7]

Unfortunately, Palés never fared as well as the poets De Onís cites. While he saw the great achievement of the later poems (section four in this book), generally critics and anthologists focussed exclusively on the Afro-Caribbean poems. There was also the double-edged consequence of their extra-literary popularity: from New York to Buenos Aires, to this day they are performed in night club routines to drumbeats—a popularity that encouraged Palés's being misread as more sound than sense. Readers hardly expected complexity in his *poemas negros,* nor a sensible discourse from his composite work.

And because racial imagery conventionally diverts literary analysis toward a narrowly social or political reading, critics also failed to appreciate that the Afro-Caribbean poems were Palés's experimentation with an anti-lyrical aesthetic. As such, in addition to what social or political discussion they might elicit, the Afro-Caribbean poems also prepared poetry readers for the humor, satire, irony and unprestigious popular speech that became the hallmark of all subsequent and, strictly speaking, *poesía negra,* which critics have failed to properly credit as the first movement in Spanish of the irony, spoken language and humor of today's Latin American poetics. In other words, in ignoring the *literary* significance of the counterpoint of his "black" and "white" poems, critics were blindsided from seeing that, as initiator of the *poesía negra* movement, Luis Palés Matos had introduced to Latin America the antipoetic aesthetic that would be popularized decades later by the Chilean Nicanor Parra[8] as *anti-poesía.*

ꞇꞗ ꞇꞗ ꞇꞗ

In the 1960s, against the backdrop of the Civil Rights Movement and the Cuban Revolution, the climate that had looked favorably on his Afro-Caribbean poems with their ostensibly superficial language play had given way to a social consciousness that preferred to hear a real black voice speaking of social and political change, namely the Afro-Cuban Nicolás Guillén. Perfecting in the thirties and forties what Palés had begun in the late twenties, Guillén's poems eschewed intricate metaphor for social realism in black talk or song and offered a clear political, social, and racial message.[9] Pitted against Guillén in the sociopolitical climate of that time, Palés seemed, to some, politically passive and an exploiter of racial imagery and themes.

But his contributions to poetry and his distinct cultural vision had yet to be discovered. Palés translated his social consciousness and cultural vision into metaphor and stylistic choices. For Palés whose politics was an expression of culture history is encoded in its politics, which is informed by determining cultural spirits that reside in language. When his sights turned to his society, therefore, he saw himself as a medium of the collective spirits that haunted his language, whether in everyday popular speech or in key totemic words (see "Kalahari," "Black Dance"). In the process, he also discovered the inauthenticities of Puerto Rican culture, which he saw as stunted by its self-deceptive sense of place and the corrupted *criollo* Spanish that his generation had inherited from the nineteenth century.

Fin de siecle decadent Romantic rhetoric contributed to this linguistic corruption. Another factor was Spain's oppressive measures to keep the remaining vestiges of its former empire. Palés's contemporary Antonio S. Pedreira argued in *Insularismo* (a book of essays on the Puerto Rican collective character, 1937) that with Spanish spies and conflicting loyalties everywhere, the general caution resulted in nineteenth-century Puerto Rican society's acquiring a penchant for euphemism and circumlocution. Pedreira labelled this collective trait *"retorismo"* and repeatedly critiqued this linguistic device that islanders used to avoid confronting harsh reality squarely. In the opening sentence to his preface, Pedreira forewarns the reader: "These words will lack that admiring tone that our complacency has created to measure our reality."

Insularismo and *Tuntún* were published in the same year. Although different in genre and divergent in their interpretations of island culture, they both acknowledged Puerto Rico's failed language[10] (a signature theme of twentieth-century Puerto Rican literature), with Palés taking that discussion in a direction that Pedreira would never have gone: toward the island's African roots. According to Palés, Puerto Rican Spanish's penchant for circumventing difficult reality contributed to the *criollo*'s never coming to terms with— despite Puerto Rico's colonial history—not being a distant extension of Spain but a culture of the Caribbean. This confusion, according to Palés, beats at the core of Puerto Rico's self-denial. Consequently, in his bittersweet "Festive Song to Be Wept," a compendium of metaphors representing each of the Caribbean islands, Palés metaphorically reduces Puerto Rico to the African-derived word *"burundanga"* (a hodgepodge), and later equates the culture to its dulcet, euphemizing language, where "life glides/ on custard phrases/ and succulent metaphors" and in which only the mad "Don Quixote," symbolizing the *criollo,* "fabricates a Dulcinea" out of the island's "Maritornes whoring."

Against the *criollo*'s denying, oblique or euphemistic, formal Spanish, then, Palés came to value the spoken diction's richer, revealing poetic ambiguity or an uncovering bluntness, an idiom infused with the genius of the island's black heritage. Over the centuries, the wit of this socially marginalized Spanish flourished in the lyrics of the *plena* and the *bomba,* two of the island's original musical forms, and eventually seeped into its general speech to produce Boricua. (From the island's indigenous name, Borikén or the latter-day Borinquen; the popular epithet for "Puerto Rican" is "Boricua.") This informal Spanish, which in the 1920s and 1930s was hardly considered suitable for serious literature, offered Palés new rhythms, fresh imagery, and an openness to nakedly see his culture in its true Latin American context. For Palés, Boricua embodied what he called the island's *numen,* its authentic genius.

∾ ∾ ∾

Luis Palés Matos grew up in the predominantly black, coastal town of Guayama. The son of a poet father and a mother who was a teacher, as a boy he was cared for by black women—domestic help cheaply available in the poverty of those times—who would take him along as they socialized in their world. Thus, it is safe to assume that his curiosity about Afro-Puerto Rican language and culture preceded his interest in literature. Equally as important, he was born in 1898, the year that, as a result of the Spanish-American War, Puerto Rico became a possession of the United States. This meant that his generation was the first that had to define Puerto Rican culture in the face of U.S. efforts to Anglicize it. When he emerged as a poet, however, his having grown up in a town nicknamed *"el pueblo de los brujos"* (the town of witch doctors) caused him to respond to the cultural threat differently from the writers and intellectuals of San Juan.

When Palés arrived at the capital, the cultural agenda had been set: as the United States promoted English, the island's intelligentsia campaigned to preserve Spanish as Puerto Rico's language and Spain as its cultural model. In academe, the "Hispanist" reaction produced a generation of prominent specialists in Spanish literature (best represented in the United States by the late critic and translator Angel Flores). During the Spanish Civil War, this Hispanist generation also welcomed exiled Spanish intellectuals, writers and artists. The two most notable were Juan Ramón Jiménez, who took up residence in his wife's homeland, where he lived when he won the Nobel Prize, and the worldrenowned cellist Pablo Casals, whose mother was Puerto Rican.

While the presence of those two great artists markedly enhanced the island's cultural life, like the Hispanist movement that paved their arrival, the heightened Spanish consciousness threatened the uniqueness of Puerto Rico's already beleaguered culture. Palés's publishing *Tuntún* in 1937, the year after the start of the Spanish Civil War, can well be interpreted, as many have, as his affirmation of Spanish against efforts to replace it with English. But the publication of a book "of island ingredients" also suggests that Palés was responding to Hispanism's losing sight of Puerto Rico's distinctly Caribbean identity.

This argument follows from Palés's Pan-Caribbean vision. According to Palés, throughout Caribbean history the overseeing island *criollos* exploited the land but refused to become one with it. Nostalgically bound to Europe, which in Palés's day was considered in decline, *criollo* culture survived as stagnant and exhausted ("Pueblo"). For the African, on the other hand, the Caribbean was a mirror of his past: a lush green temple. Africans worked the land and in the process sowed their ancestral spirits and gods. In time, the indigenous Caribbean peoples having disappeared, Africans, being at home with the climate and their portable gods, became the new indigene and their spirits gave the land its unique character. For this reason, however much *criollos* imagined they lived on island-scale models of provinces of Spain or France or England, the Caribbean's distinctive *numen* or defining spirit became black, and according to Palés, even white islanders's souls were embued with African spirits that informed their collective psyche and their language.

Palés did not come to this vision all at once, having to evolve away from ingrained *criollo* racial attitudes. Although it is impossible to trace the exact chronology of these poems,[11] which Palés worked and reworked while starting others, we can extrapolate a trajectory of stages in three versions of his vision of a *pueblo negro* (black town). The earliest was a prose piece, a paragraph titled "*Pueblo de Negros*" (Town of Blacks), which describes his walk through a black town. This paragraph has little worth noting except that his description objectifies the town as strange and exotic to him.

The second version, "Esta Noche He Pasado" (Tonight I Have Passed), added a subtle racist, jocular nuance in the title: *Pasado* plays with *pasa*, kinky hair—hair being a defining feature of blackness in the Hispanic Caribbean. But there is more to the word play: "*He Pasado*" says that he both passes through the town and as well "passes for" black. The title, in addition to illustrating his inability to resist a pun, also highlights the poet's immersion in the town. From there, the poem describes his walk through the town, and as in the earlier piece, underscores a mutual exoticism. But this poem ends with the poet's envisioning the townspeople's African past, concluding with a catalogue of underlying "combustible" forces that he perceived in their black eyes: "tar,/ diamond, coal, hatred and the mountain." Both evocations, the African past and the combustible forces, foreshadow what in later poems Palés will call the black *numen*.

"Pueblo Negro" (Black Town), written around six years later, is about his uttering the names of real African towns, "Mussumba, Tombuctú, Farafangana," which evoke in him a "dreamstuff" black town. The mirror image of a coastal Caribbean town, somewhere in it a black woman is singing. In fact, we soon realize, the dream medium in which the town materializes is her song, which is also metaphorically described as emanating from her womb. Listening to her song, the poet is struck by the lyric's exotic-sounding "gutturals," "diphthongs," and notably, the drumlike u-sound (pronounced like the English "oo," as in too), a sound that recurs in Spanish sex-related words and that also evokes a drumbeat (*tuntún*). As the woman's song fades, the dream town disappears until all that remains in the poet's soul is the visualized "u" (oo), "whose maternal curve secretes/ the prolific harmony of sex." The latent, combustible force that Palés first saw in exotic Afro-Caribbean eyes had evolved into a sensual music spread by a numinous black woman muse singing in his language and his soul.

This maturing of consciousness culminates in Palés's finally embracing the mulatta ("Mulatta-Antille") as symbol of the mingled African and European cultures of the Caribbean: "In you, mulatta, I now embrace. . . ." But even though this celebration contains a discourse on race, Palés's thematic emphasis was actually on the mingling of spirits, genius or force. Owing to this spirituality, Palés's poetry did not strictly adhere to the conventions of racially-themed poetry. Unlike the black Nicolás Guillén, for example, Palés did not write socio-political testimonial. And, despite his detractors's misreadings of his work, neither did he write in blackface. His Afro-Caribbean poems are testimonials on his reconciling contradictory Spanish and African spirits; they are lyrical narratives on the Caribbean spiritual drama, epitomized, according to Palés, by the constant conflict between an African cult to sensuality, with its immediate contact with the spiritual world, and a Western cult to sexual abstention and religious formula and hierarchy.

This spiritual consciousness threads his "white" and "black" poems. On closer reading of his non-Afro-Caribbean poems, we discover that although they are less ornate in sound effects and exotic imagery, they too are reflections on the numinous essence of things but translated into the conventional language of love and metaphysical inquiry. If the critics failed to trace this common nerve between Palés's "black" and "white" poetry, it was because they were not prepared to read in the Afro-Caribbean poetry the kind of discourse not regularly associated with racial imagery. Also, to Palés's misfortune, the Afro-Caribbean poetry was *too* effectively rhythmic and its wordplay *too* humorous. As a result, few critics caught on that he was serious about possessing an Afro-Caribbean consciousness.

The marker of his sincerity, however, is the unifying spiritual or metaphysical theme. Until he started writing the Afro-Caribbean poems, his work was structured to celebrate a Western, Aristotelian body-soul dualism; after adopting a Caribbean consciousness, the traditional dualism was dropped, and his poems celebrated animism, painting his Caribbean world as haunted with re-emerging manifestations of its Spanish and African numina in cyclical time. In fact, even as the Afro-Caribbean poems articulated Palés's cultural vision, they were also a stage of his personal odyssey, phases that can be read as a meandering journey in search of spiritual authenticity.

ᑲᏉ ᑲᏉ ᑲᏉ

His early poetry, influenced by theosophy, contemplated the body's connection to the soul and reality's border with poetry ("The Pool," "The Unknown Sorrow").[12] With his poetic maturity came a curiosity about words as totems ("Numen"), language as time ("Pueblo Negro"), and a collective unconscious latent in words

("Kalahari"). In his last phase, the metaphysical discourse is central and reveals that the link between the voices that critics had called "white" and "black" was the notion of the "numen," first used in the Afro-Caribbean poems: like the numina that inspirit and inform the Caribbean, his personal "numen" was poetry.

In that last phase, two important poems, "Entrance to Time in Three Voices" and "The Killer Pursuit," form part of a cycle in which he describes his lifelong pursuit of Filí-Melé,[13] his personification of the essence of poetry. All his life as poet he had pursued her and fleetingly possessed her in the process of writing, only to inevitably lose her. That cycle both drained and replenished his life. Now, aging, he yearned to have her again, but his "numen" had become even more elusive. He also realized that all along she, poetry, was also the essence of Being, of which we can only fleetingly glimpse, have a vague sense:

> In what is fleeting, in what ceases to exist
> while being thought
> and the instant no longer thought
> exists again;
> in what if named is shattered,
> cathedral of ashes, tree of mist . . .
> How to climb to your branch?
> How to knock at your door?

It is in the context of this philosophical bent in Palés that we must read the Afro-Caribbean poems. Besides what cultural or racial curiosity Palés also had in Afro-Caribbean things, his aspiring to a Heideggerian authenticity in contemplating his Being also informed his search for the essential Hispanic Caribbean spirit. This defining "numen," he envisioned, was a composite of Spanish and African numina ("Not This, Not That"), a spiritual mingling. It is that mingling of Spanish and African spirit that gives Hispanic Caribbean culture its unique character, and inspirits the Caribbean people regardless of skin color. Confronted by the implications of such a provocative idea, admirers of Palés highlighted his humor, wordplay, and strong rhythms but failed to see them as devices used to sensorially color a cultural vision that emanates from his personal spiritual consciousness.

Palés, for example, humorously contemplated the theological dilemma of a spiritual mingling on earth of white and black cultures while, according to the iconography, the Western God is implicitly white. This is the premise of "*Ñáñigo* to Heaven," in which a *ñáñigo* (a member of an Afro-Cuban sect) is ascending to Western culture's Heaven, a place inhabited by white souls. To welcome the newcomer, Heaven is bedecked to resemble the tropics. The heavenly beings behave as absurd and racially self-conscious as on earth. Ultimately, however, those celestial beings are infected by the *ñáñigo*'s music and dance as, in a secret agreement between the charismatic black soul and the white God, the *ñáñigo* becomes a Caribbean numen.[14]

A nuance of Palés's obsession with authenticity is his idealization of the primal, which he equated with the spiritual and condensed in animal metaphors. Thus, his heart is described as a frog, his animus is compared to a broken-down horse, the Caribbean to a phallic gamecock, and sailors have eyes like meek oxen. Problematically, he also uses the ape both to romanticize a freer, natural, noble spirit within the black and to mock the mimicking, colonized black man who assumes the rituals of the white man. Such simian imagery can be and has been denounced as racist, but as Palés's treatment is not that simple ("*Ñáñigo* to Heaven" and "Shake-It Plena"), neither can we rush to pronounce judgment on his use of simian imagery.

"Elegy for the Duke of Marmalade," a parody of Henri Christophe's mulatto court, derides the Duke for adopting French social formulas at the expense of the freer spirit of his African ancestry. Palés borrows that African setting of the Duke's numinous past from travelogue literature about the then-perceived *Dark Continent:*

Oh my fine, my honey-colored Duke of Marmalade!
Where are your crocodiles in the far-off village on the Pongo,
and the round blue shadow of your African baobabs, •
and your fifteen wives smelling of mud and the jungle?

The second stanza describes the Duke's former self as groomed by the "family monkey" and of a cannibal nature that eats roasted children. The hyperbole satirizes the white image of Africans but can also be read as racist, especially as the poem subsequently urges the

Duke to free his primal being from the trappings of Dukedom: ". . . climb up to the cornices of the palace."

In the final stanza, however, the poem undergoes an important change in tone:

> From the farthest shores of your great great-grandfather,
> across the hot flat silence of the plains,
> why do your crocodiles weep in the far-off village on the
> Pongo,
> Oh my fine, my honey-colored Duke of Marmalade?

The word "fine," ironically used in the first stanza, loses its sarcastic edge. Now what makes the Duke "fine" is his spiritual pedigree, his long lost ancestral numina, for whom his crocodiles weep what are intended to be genuine and not crocodile tears. Evoking a nostalgia for (Palés's idealized perception of) the Duke's authentic, primal self, the final stanza makes us reread the early simian imagery in a different, if romantic light.

"Elegía," then, must be read in the context of Palés's reconciling his conflictive linguistic and spiritual legacies: his *criollo* persona weaned on racist preconceptions and ignoring racial realities; his Afro-Caribbean consciousness that despised black capitulators to white assumptions. One may argue that a racist tinge mars his ascribing, for whatever reason, a more genuine simian or savage nature to the Duke as opposed, say, to his own nature. For this there is no counterargument as Palés—not a person of our supposedly enlightened times, and who would sell his mother for a joke—sometimes does reveal vestiges of *criollo* attitudes. And still, Palés perceived poetry itself as a primal force that, in his Caribbean case, he believed was nourished by his African cultural heritage. In one of his youthful poems, "My Poem" (not included in this selection), he envisions himself as "wild, jungle-born like a proud savage" whose poetry "grinds out the sensation/ of a fang being honed on a sharp rock . . ." For this reason, it is important to remind the reader that this satirizing or even ironic celebration of popular preconceptions of those who are "jungle-born," no matter how simian they are portrayed, was being done by a poet who pronounced his culture as redeemed by its African heritage.

Similarly, one may oversimplify Palés's portrayal of women. Palés's attitudes reflected those of his time, and in his poems women are never represented as flesh and blood beings or individuated psyches but as metaphors. In some poems, these women embody primal forces depicted in animal metaphors. A young country woman, for example, stares "bovinely." The black woman in "Pueblo Negro" sings of her life of a "domestic animal." But in all cases that primal force is creative in every sense of the word, making them all simultaneously mothers, lovers and muses—incarnations of spiritual essence, the spirit made flesh but ever on the verge of returning to spirit. Consequently, all his women metaphors inevitably dissolve into a spreading atmosphere or spirit or redolence that infuses the power of sensuality, procreation and regeneration.

Among these metaphors, the socially impure and therefore liberated mulatta reigns as his symbol of political and sexual freedom. In "Mulatta-Antille," the numinous, scandalously dancing mulatta—whose sensual, swaying body is the Caribbean Sea—is described as "Liberty in song in the Antilles." The goddess Tembandumba in "Majestad Negra" and the dancing Island in "Shake It *Plena*" are versions of the same mulatta, and even his ethereal Filí-Melé. Although the protagonist of his later, misnomered "white" poems, Filí-Melé is celebrated for inspiriting all previous stages of his work, including the Afro-Caribbean poems; we discover that the earlier "Mulatta-Antille" was also the yet to be named "numen" and muse, Filí-Melé.

༄ ༄ ༄

Finally, although Palés Matos's work belongs to Spanish-language poetry and descends from it, very important influences also came from three Anglo-American poets. Early on and consistent with the residual (highly Frenchified) Latin American romanticism that carried over from the nineteenth century, Palés was an avid reader of Edgar Allen Poe. Combining the influence of Poe with his own readings of Jung and Freud and the theosophists, much of Palés's early poetry is set in a nocturnal dream-state, a journey into the center of his dream. Among that early work figure imitations of Poe (neither in this selection), "Dream-land" and "The Haunted Palace." Poe's influence is also evident in "Sea Song," almost two decades later, which includes the line: "remote Ulalumes of indescribable dreams."

Vachel Lindsay's ear is obvious in the Afro-Caribbean poems, with their drum effects reminiscent of *The Congo* (1914), which also doubtless encouraged Palés to turn his curiosity about African things into poetry. But *The Congo* wasn't all Palés read of Lindsay. The Anglo American poet's combination of popular speech and humor in measured, rhythmic blank verse also seemed to have a marked influence on Palés. Consequently, other, non-onomatopoeic poems by Lindsay impressed Palés. "*Ñáñigo al Cielo*" ("*Ñáñigo* Goes to Heaven"), for example, is modeled after Lindsay's "General William Booth Enters into Heaven." Moreover, Lindsay's poetry, rich with spoken language and jazz rhythms, also contributed its Americentricity. Reinforcing the lesson of Palés's *modernista* mentors, whose emergence established Latin America's literary coming of age before Spain, Lindsay's Anglo American voice contributed to Palés's developing a sense of his own Latin American place and idiom.

A third American influence was Walt Whitman. If Lindsay provided rhythmic, imagistic and thematic models, Whitman's broad American vision encouraged Palés to take a wide, panoramic view of the Caribbean and appreciate its unprestigious components. Palés, inspired to take the Afro-Caribbean component of his culture seriously, credited Whitman's "raising his weighty and orchestral massiveness in the praise of everything that previous poets would have thought sacrilegious . . . .."[15] In the 1920s, nothing could have been more sacrilegious than avowing that Puerto Rico, assumed by the dominant *criollo* to be a remote cultural province of Spain, was as much a remote spiritual province of Africa.

Like Whitman and Lindsay, Palés intended his Afro-Caribbean poetry to be impure in the sense of creating a countersong, although his rebellion resisted gravitating to Whitman's free verse, keeping instead to Lindsay's measured, rhythmic lines—a fusion of styles, Boricua diction in formal structure, that structurally celebrates the Caribbean's *mulatez*. Unfortunately, this stylistic statement went unnoticed by an age in which such intentional racial minglings, even symbolic ones, were inconceivable.

❧ Introduction ❧

Luis Palés Matos, in sum, was a house of mingled spirits that included the influence of poets from English-speaking America. So when he and William Carlos Williams met in 1941, yet another kinship connected them. Palés of the Spanish "line" was, of course, a poet in what Williams considered "the mingling," American grain, but little did William Carlos imagine that they also shared a lineage from Anglo-American poetry, a coincidence that gave even more credence to his having heard a common idiom in their different American languages.

Julio Marzán
New York

Notes

[1] He had also accepted the invitation to gather material for a biography on his mother, Elena Hoheb Williams. Many years later he wrote the experimental portrait *Yes, Mrs. Williams.*

[2] Williams wrote the word "'line'" in quotation marks, to signal its intentional artistic/ genealogical ambiguity. For more on Williams's interest in his background, see *The Spanish American Roots of William Carlos Williams* (University of Texas, 1994).

[3] Cubism, according to Picasso, was inspired by the poetry of Góngora.

[4] The poem addresses the transmitter of his "strange courage," literally an "ancient star," which etymologically encodes "old Helen," his mother, but Góngora too was another kind of "ancient star." "Strange courage" etymologically encodes "foreign heart."

[5] For a more detailed analysis of Palés's work, see my *The Numinous Site: the Poetry of Luis Palés Matos* (Madison: Associated University Presses, 1995).

[6] *Historia de la Literatura Latinoamericana,* 6th ed. México: Fondo de Cultura Económica, 1954, 189.

[7] In his preface to Palés's *Poesías 1915-1956* (1957).

[8] For a complete discussion of this thesis, see "The Poetry and Antipoetry of Luis Palés Matos: From *Canciones* to *Tuntunes,"* in *Callaloo,* Volume 18, Number 2.

[9] Indeed Guillén was perhaps the earliest true *poeta comunicante,* as in the 1970s the Uruguayan Mario Benedetti would call that generation of conversational anti-lyrical poets, overlooking Afro-Caribbean poetry's role in the evolution.

[10] This discussion has nothing to do with the U.S. imposition of English on Puerto Rico.

[11] I consulted Mercedes López-Baralt's critical edition of *La poesía de Luis Palés Matos* (University of Puerto Rico Press, 1995) for publication dates.

[12] Despite appearances, this poetry was also a private "countersong": his atheist father died, as Williams recounts the legend, in the act of reading a poem against the Creator.

[13] Phonetically a combination of heavy and dynamic sounds, Filí Melé was a nickname that Palés, then an old man, gave to a young *mulata* with whom he fell in love.

[14] This imagery can be facilely misread as racist—the *ñáñigo* as a dancing spirit—but we must remember that "having rhythm" has a different connotation in the Caribbean, the birthplace of most popular Latin dance music. In "Shake It Plena," Palés urges the *mulatta*-island to "shake it, shake it" because that ability to dance and be sinful will save her from the morally stiff-hipped, ogling "Mister" from across the ocean.

[15] Luis Palés Matos, "Intelectual Puertorriqueño," from *Los Quijotes,* San Juan, P.R., 17 November 1927, in *Poesía Completa y Prosa Selecta,* ed. Margot Arce de Vázquez (Caracas: Ayacucho, 1978), 211.

Part I

1920-1925

Claro de Luna

En la noche de luna, en esta noche
de luna clara y tersa,
mi corazón como una rana oscura
salta sobre la hierba.

¡Qué alegre está mi corazón ahora!
¡Con qué gusto levanta la cabeza
bajo el claro de luna pensativo
esta medrosa rana de tragedia!

Arriba, por los árboles,
las aves blandas sueñan
y más arriba aún, sobre las nubes,
recién lavadas brillan las estrellas . . .

¡Ah, que no llegue nunca la mañana!
¡Que se alargue esta lenta
hora de beatitud en que las cosas
adquieren una irrealidad suprema;

y en que mi corazón, como una rana,
se sale de sus ciénagas,
y se va bajo el claro de la luna
en vuelo sideral por las estrellas!

Moonlight

In full-moon night, in this night's
brightly polished moon,
like a dark frog, my heart
leaps onto the grass.

How happy my heart feels right now!
How joyfully it lifts its head
musing in the moonlight,
this shy, tragedian frog!

High in the branches,
gentle birds are dreaming,
and higher, beyond clouds,
just-washed gleam the stars . . .

Ah, let morning never come!
Never end, drowsy hour,
in whose bliss things assume
a supreme dream-reality;

when my heart like a frog
emerges from its swamp
and takes off in moonlight
on a star's flight among the stars!

El Pozo

Mi alma es como un pozo de agua sorda y profunda
en cuya paz solemne e imperturbable ruedan
los días, apagando sus rumores mundanos
en la quietud que cuajan las oquedades muertas.

Abajo el agua pone su claror de agonía:
irisación morbosa que en las sombras fermenta;
linfas que se coagulan en largos limos negros
y exhalan esta exangüe y azul fosforescencia.

Mi alma es como un pozo. El paisaje dormido
turbiamente en el agua se forma y se dispersa,
y abajo, en lo más hondo, hace tal vez mil años,
una rana misántropa y agazapada sueña.

A veces al influjo lejano de la luna
el pozo adquiere un vago prestigio de leyenda;
se oye el cró-cró profundo de la rana en el agua,
y un remoto sentido de eternidad lo llena.

The Well

My soul is like a well of deaf, deep water
on whose solemn, unrippled peace
days wheel, drowning their daily murmur
in the calm that curdles in barren hollows.

Below, the water lays its agony brightness,
a feeble iridescence fermenting in darkness;
lymphs that clot into long black slime
and exude this bloodless blue phosphoresence.

My soul is like a well. The sleepy water landscape
trembling composes itself and disperses,
while below, fathoms, perhaps a thousand years back,
dreams a crouched, misanthropic frog.

At times under the moon's long influence,
the well displays the misty magic of a fable:
a frog's deep croaking echoes in its water,
and it brims with a faint sense of eternity.

El Dolor Desconocido

Hoy me he dado a pensar en el dolor lejano
que sentirá mi carne, allá en sus aposentos
y arrabales remotos que se quedan a oscuras
en su mundo de sombras y de instintos espesos.
A veces, de sus roncos altamares ocultos,
de esas inexploradas distancias, vienen ecos
tan vagos, que se pierden como ondas desmayadas
sobre una playa inmóvil de bruma y de silencio.
Son mensajes que llegan desesperadamente
del ignorado fondo de estos dramas secretos:
gritos de auxilio, voces de socorro, gemidos,
cual de un navío enorme que naufraga a lo lejos.

¡Oh esos limbos hundidos en tinieblas cerradas;
esos desconocidos horizontes internos
que subterráneamente se alargan en nosotros
distantes de las zonas de luz del pensamiento!
Quizás las más profundas tragedias interiores,
los más graves sucesos,
pasan en estos mudos arrabales de sombra
sin que llegue a nosotros el más vago lamento,
y tal vez, cuando estamos riendo a carcajadas,
somos el tenebroso escenario grotesco
de ese horrible dolor que no tiene respuesta
y cuya voz inútil se pierde sobre el viento.

The Unknown Sorrow

All today I thought of the distant sorrow
my flesh must feel, away in its remote
houses and slums damned to darkness,
their shadow world of packed instincts.
At times from its roaring, hidden high seas,
those uncharted leagues, arrive echoes so faint
they die like waves too weak to crest
on a beach congealed in fog and silence.
They are calls that franticly flee
the unknown depths of these secret dramas:
cries for help, screams for aid, groans as if
a colossal ship were wrecked far off.

Oh those limbos submerged in trapped night,
those unimagined inner horizons
extending underground inside us,
beyond the mind's radius of light!
Maybe the saddest interior tragedies,
the most heartbreaking events
take place in those mute shadow slums
as we hear not the faintest moan,
and maybe when we laugh till we cry,
we are the bleak, grotesque setting
of that monstrous, inconsolable sorrow,
whose useless voice is lost in the wind.

Topografía

Esta es la tierra estéril y madrastra
en donde brota el cacto.
Salitral blanquecino que atraviesa
roto de sed el pájaro;
con marismas resecas espaciadas
a extensos intérvalos,
y un cielo fijo, inalterable y mudo,
cubriendo todo el ámbito.

El sol calienta en las marismas rojas
el agua como un caldo,
y arranca al arenal caliginoso
un brillo seco y áspero.
La noche cierra pronto y en el lúgubre
silencio rompe el sapo
su grito de agua oculta que las sombras
absorben como tragos.

Miedo. Desolación. Asfixia. Todo
duerme aquí sofocado
bajo la línea muerta que recorta
el ras rígido y firme de los campos.
Algunas cabras amarillas medran
en el rastrojo escaso,
y en la distancia un buey rumia su sueño
turbio de soledad y de cansancio.

Esta es la tierra estéril y madrastra.
Cunde un tufo malsano
de cosa descompuesta en la marisma
por el fuego que baja de lo alto;
fermento tenebroso que en la noche
arroja el fuego fatuo,
y da esas largas formas fantasmales
que se arrastran sin ruido sobre el páramo.

Topography

This is the barren, stepmother land
where cactus blooms.
Hoary saltpeter birds fly over
brittle with thirst;
parched marshes here and there
over wide reaches,
and a constant sky, relentless and mute,
doming all the region.

In red marshes, the sun
heats the water to a broth,
extracting from dark sand
a dry, craggy shine.
Night falls soon, and in dismal silence
toads begin their croak
like unseen water that shadows
gulp like drinks.

Fear. Desolation. Asphysixia. Everything
sleeps smothered
under the languid line that cuts
the country's rigid, cast skyline.
A few yellow goats graze
on sparse stubble, and far off an ox,
vexed with solitude and fatigue,
chews the cud of his dream.

This is the barren, stepmother land.
Everywhere a sickly stench,
something the hail of fire
putrefies in the bog,
a dark fermentation that at night
flashes the will-o-the-wisp
that sends those long phantasmal forms
shuffling without sound over the plain.

Esta es la tierra donde vine al mundo.
—Mi infancia ha ramoneado
como una cabra arisca por el yermo
rencoroso y misántropo—.
Esta es toda mi historia:
sal, aridez, cansancio
una vaga tristeza indefinible,
una inmóvil fijeza de pantano,
y un grito, allá en el fondo,
como un hongo terrible y obstinado,
cuajándose entre fofas carnaciones
de inútiles deseos apagados.

On this land I entered the world.
—Like a surly goat
over the mean, recluse desert,
my early years grazed on twigs and branches.
My entire history is this:
salt, dryness, fatigue,
a vague, amorphous sorrow,
a dormant, swamp's constancy
and a scream, deepest down,
like a fierce, unstoppable mushroom
puffing among spongy corpses
of useless, stillborn desires.

de *Los Animales Interiores*

I

Ese caballo está dentro de mí, ese viejo
caballo que la lluvia—mustio violín—alarga,
igual que sobre un lienzo crepuscular lo miro
proyectarse hacia el vago fondo de mi nostalgia.

A la fábrica en ruinas de su cuerpo la lluvia
se arropa mansamente como una hiedra elástica,
y al caer sosegado de las gotas, derrumba
la frente y las tupidas orejas se le apagan.

Sus patas, sus ollares, el ensueño perdido
que en sus ojos de bestia pura y simple naufraga,
toda esa mansedumbre derrengada y maltrecha,
ese sexo en silencio, esas crines chorreadas,

todo tiene una exangüe repercusión interna,
que la lluvia con blandos bemoles acompaña,
y me veo un caballo fantasmal y remoto
allá en una pluviosa lejanía de alma.

from *The Animals Within*

I

That horse is inside me, that old
horse the rain—whining violin—paints longer,
as if on a twilight canvas I see it
cast against the gray background of my longing.

Around its abandoned-factory body
rain wraps supplely as an elastic vine,
and under the calm fall of drops, its forelock
droops and its clogged ears hear nothing.

Its legs, its nostrils, the lost dream
shipwrecked in its pure, simple beast eyes,
all that abused, broken docility,
that silenced sex, that streaming mane,

its whole body one bloodless internal beat
that raindrops accompany in soft flats,
as I see myself a horse, ghostly and far,
away in a rainy outback of soul.

Pueblo

¡Piedad, Señor, piedad para mi pobre pueblo
donde mi pobre gente se morirá de nada!
Aquel viejo notario que se pasa los días
en su mínima y lenta preocupación de rata;
este alcalde adiposo de grande abdomen vacuo
chapoteando en su vida tal como en una salsa;
aquel comercio lento, igual, de hace diez siglos;
estas cabras que triscan al resol de la plaza;
algún mendigo, algún caballo que atraviesa
tiñoso, gris y flaco, por estas calles anchas;
la fría y atrofiante modorra del domingo
jugando en los casinos con billar y barajas;
todo, todo el rebaño tedioso de estas vidas
en este pueblo viejo donde no ocurre nada,
todo esto se muere, se cae, se desmorona,
a fuerza de ser cómodo y estar a sus anchas.

¡Piedad, Señor, piedad para mi pobre pueblo!
Sobre estas almas simples, desata algún canalla
que contra el agua muerta de sus vidas arroje
la piedra redentora de una insólita hazaña . . .
Algún ladrón que asalte ese Banco en la noche,
algún don Juan que viole esa doncella casta,
algún tahur de oficio que se meta en el pueblo
y revuelva estas gentes honorables y mansas.

¡Piedad, Señor, piedad para mi pobre pueblo
donde mi pobre gente se morirá de nada!

Town

Pity, Lord, pity on my poor town
where my poor people will likely die of nothing.
That old notary who devotes his days
to his slow, detailed, rat's worries;
this fat mayor, huge his vacuous paunch,
dabbling in his life as if in a sauce;
that store with few customers, unchanged for ten centuries;
those goats frisking in the plaza sun,
a beggar, a bony horse, scabby and gray,
clomping along these wide streets;
the cold, grinding boredom of Sundays
shooting pool and playing cards in bars;
Everything, the whole tedious herd of these lives
in this old town where nothing happens,
all this dies, falls, collapses
from living easy and content with one's lot.

Pity, Lord, pity on my poor town.
Over these simple souls, unleash some rogue
who'd hurl against their dead-water lives
the liberating stone of an impulsive act . . .
Some thief to break open that Bank in the night,
some Don Juan to seduce that chaste young lady,
some professional cardshark to enter the town
and shuffle these honorable, docile people.

Pity, Lord, pity on my poor town
where my poor people will likely die of nothing.

Nocturno

El panorama es turbio bajo la luna acuosa
que pone un submarino claror sobre los árboles.
Trasnocho. Por las anchas alamedas en blanco,
no va ni viene nadie.

El silencio es tan hondo y las cosas están
tan sensibles, tan vagas, tan aéreas, tan frágiles,
que si yo diera un grito caerían las estrellas
húmedas sobre el parque.

Hay que estar quieto, quieto, pues cualquier ademán
tendría una alargada repercusión unánime . . .
—Como una gota densa y profunda, en la noche,
la hora, remota, cae.

Nocturne

The view is blurry under aquatic moonlight
coating the trees with an underwater glaze.
I stay up all night. Along the wide blank walk
no one comes nor goes.

So deep is the silence, and things appear
so delicate, so formless, so aerial, so frail,
that if I were to let out a scream
wet stars would hail on the park.

One has to freeze, freeze, for any gesture
can cause one long unanimous consequence . . .
—Like a heavy ocean drop in the night,
the hour, somewhere distant, falls.

Part II

1926-1937

Preludio en Boricua

Tuntún de pasa y grifería
y otros parejeros tuntunes.
Bochinche de ñañiguería
donde sus cálidos betunes
funde la congada bravía.

Con cacareo de maraca
y sordo gruñido de gongo,
el telón isleño destaca
una aristocracia macaca
a base de funche y mondongo.

Al solemne papaluá haitiano
opone la rumba habanera
sus esguinces de hombro y cadera,
mientras el negrito cubano
doma la mulata cerrera.

De su bachata por las pistas
vuela Cuba, suelto el velamen,
recogiendo en el caderamen
su áureo niágara de turistas.

(Mañana serán accionistas
de cualquier ingenio cañero
y cargarán con el dinero . . .)

Y hacia un rincón—solar, bahía,
malecón o siembra de cañas—
bebe el negro su pena fría
alelado en la melodía
que le sale de las entrañas.

Prelude in Boricua

Tomtom of kinky hair and black things
and other, uppity tomtoms.
Secret Cuban buzz-buzz
where the savage drumming
casts its hot shoeblacking.

To rattles of maracas
and *gongos's* muffled grunts,
the Caribbean curtain rises
on a macaque aristocracy
rich in cornmeal and tripe.

Haiti's solemn voodoo priest
Havana counters with rumba,
shaking shoulders and hips
while the Cuban darkie
saddles his wild mulatta.

Her dance-floor swing
propels Cuba at full sail,
her big hips drawing in
its golden tourist Niagara.

(Tomorrow they'll invest
in whatever sugar mill
and run home with the loot . . .)

And off in a corner—basement, bay,
seaside walk or cane field—
the black man sips his sorrow cold
high on the melody
seeping from his core.

Jamaica, la gorda mandinga,
reduce su lingo a gandinga.
Santo Domingo se endominga
y en cívico gesto imponente
su numen heroico respinga
con cien odas al Presidente.
Con su batea de ajonjolí
y sus blancos ojos de magia
hacia el mercado viene Haití.
Las antillas barloventeras
pasan tremendas desazones,
espantándose los ciclones
con matamoscas de palmeras.

¿Y Puerto Rico? Mi isla ardiente,
para ti todo ha terminado.
En el yermo de un continente,
Puerto Rico, lúgubremente,
bala como cabro estofado.

Tuntún de Pasa y Grifería,
este libro que va a tus manos
con ingredientes antillanos
compuse un día . . .

. . . y en resumen, tiempo perdido,
que me acaba en aburrimiento.
Algo entrevisto o presentido,
poco realmente vivido
y mucho de embuste y de cuento.

Jamaica, the fat Mandingo
makes liver stew of her lingo.
Santo Domingo dons his best suit
and in an awesome civic gesture,
wincing, his heroic numen recites
one hundred odes to the President.*
Bearing a tray of sesame,
with white magical eyes
Haiti comes to market.
The wind-whipped Antilles
great hardships endure,
trying to scare off cyclones
with palm-tree swatters.

And Puerto Rico? My fevered island,
for you the party's over.
In the wasteland of a continent,
mournfully Puerto Rico
bleats like a stewed goat.

Tomtom of Kinky Hair and Black Things,
this book that puts in your hands
island ingredients,
I compiled one day . . .

. . . and in sum, time wasted,
whose last page is boredom.
Things glimpsed or envisioned,
scant actually lived,
and much concoction and fable.

*Rafael Trujillo (1891-1961) was the legendarily ruthless dictator of the Dominican
  Republic.

Canción Festiva para Ser Llorada

Cuba—ñáñigo y bachata—
Haití—vodú y calabaza—
Puerto Rico—burundanga—

Martinica y Guadalupe
me van poniendo la casa.
Martinica en la cocina
y Guadalupe en la sala.
Martinica hace la sopa
y Guadalupe la cama.
Buen calalú, Martinica,
que Guadalupe me aguarda.

¿En qué lorito aprendiste
ese patuá de melaza,
Guadalupe de mis trópicos,
mi suculenta tinaja?
A la francesa, resbalo,
sobre tu carne mulata,
que a falta de pan, tu torta
es prieta gloria antillana.
He de traerte de Haití
un cónsul de aristocracia:
Conde del Aro en la Oreja,
Duque de la Mermelada.

Para cuidarme el jardín
con Santo Domingo basta.
Su perenne do de pecho
pone intrusos a distancia.
Su agrio gesto de primate
en lira azul azucara,
cuando borda madrigales
con dedos de butifarra.

Festive Song to Be Wept

Cuba—*ñáñigos* and good times—
Haiti—voodoo and gourds—
Puerto Rico—a hodgepodge—

Martinique and Guadalupe
keep my house in order.
Martinique in the kitchen,
Guadalupe in the parlor.
Martinique heats my soup,
Guadalupe my bed.
Cook a good *callaloo,* Martinique,
Guadalupe is waiting.

What little parrot taught you
that molasses patois,
my tropical Guadalupe,
my succulent pottage.
In the French style I slide
over your mulatta flesh
as, not having bread, your torte's
a dark Caribbean treat.
From Haiti I'll bring you
an aristocratic consul:
Count Ring in the Ear,
the Duke of Marmelade.

To tend to my garden
Santo Domingo will do.
His constant, extreme effort
keeps intruders at bay.
His bitter primate grimace
sweetens to blue poem
when he embroiders madrigals
with dark sausage fingers.

Cuba—ñáñigo y bachata—
Haití—vodú y calabaza—
Puerto Rico—burundanga—

Las antillas menores,
titís inocentes, bailan
sobre el ovillo de un viento
que el ancho golfo huracana.

Aquí está St. Kitts el nene,
el bobo de la comarca.
Pescando tiernos ciclones
entretiene su ignorancia.
Los purga con sal de fruta,
los ceba con cocos de agua,
y adultos ya, los remite,
C.O.D. a sus hermanas,
para que se desayunen
con tormenta rebozada.

Aquí está Santo Tomé,
de malagueta y malanga
cargado el burro que el cielo
de Su Santidad demanda . . .
(Su Santidad, Babbit Máximo,
con sello y marca de fábrica).
De su grave teología
Lutero hizo una fogata,
y alrededor, biblia en mano,
los negros tórtolos bailan
cantando salmos oscuros
a Bombo, mongo de África.

¡Hola, viejo Curazao!
Ya yo te he visto la cara.
Tu bravo puño de hierro
me ha quemado la garganta.

Cuba—*ñáñigos* and good times—
Haiti—voodoo and gourds—
Puerto Rico—a hodgepodge—

The smaller antilles,
guileless baby monkeys,
prance atop a whirlwind
the wide gulf whips to a hurricane.

Here St. Kitts the kid,
the village idiot.
Netting young cyclones,
he entertains his ignorance.
He purges them with fruit salt,
he fattens them on coconut,
and once they grow full-blown,
sends them C.O.D.
so his sisters may savor
breakfast of basted storm.

Here comes St. Thomas,
burro under the weight
of tubers and hot peppers
His Holiness mandates . . .
(His Holiness, Supreme Babbitt,
with brand name and seal).
With his severe theology
Luther sparked a bonfire,
and round it, holding bibles,
Tortola blacks dance
singing dark psalms
to Bombo, chief of Africa.

Hi, old Curaçao!
You're no stranger to me.
Your fiery iron fist
has blazed down my throat.

Por el mundo, embotellado,
vas del brazo de Jamaica,
soltando tu áspero tufo
de azúcares fermentadas.

Cuba—ñáñigo y bachata—
Haití—vodú y calabaza—
Puerto Rico—burundanga—

Mira que te coge el ñáñigo,
niña, no salgas de casa.
Mira que te coge el ñáñigo
del juegito de la Habana.
Con tu carne hará gandinga,
con tu seso mermelada;
ñáñigo carabalí
de la manigua cubana.

Me voy al titiringó
de la calle de la prángana,
ya verás el huele-huele
que enciendo tras de mi saya,
cuando resude canela
sobre la rumba de llamas;
que a mí no me arredra el ñáñigo
del jueguito de la Habana.

Macandal bate su gongo
en la torva noche haitiana.
Dentaduras de marfil
en la tiniebla resaltan.
Por los árboles se cuelan
ariscas formas extrañas,
y Haití, fiero y enigmático,
hierve como una amenaza.

Bottled you span the world
are-in-arm with Jamaica,
giving off your pungent
fermented-sugar smell.

Cuba—*ñáñigos* and good times—
Haiti—voodoo and gourds—
Puerto Rico—a hodgepodge—

"Stay away from the *ñáñigo,*
girl, don't leave the house.
Stay away from the *ñáñigo*
of that bad Havana sect.
With your flesh he'll make a stew,
with your brains a marmalade,
that Carabar-blooded ñáñigo
of the Cuban bush."

"I'm off to the big bash
on the dead-end street,
soon you'll smell the heat
I'll ignite under my skirt
when I'm sweatin' cinnamon
over the rumba in flames
'cause that Havana-sect ñáñigo,
he don't frighten me."

Macandal beats his drum
in Haiti's scary night.
Glowing marble teeth
grin in the dark.
Eerie beastly forms
creep in the treetops,
and primal, intricate Haiti
simmers like a threat.

Es el vodú. La tremenda
hora del zombí y la rana.
Sobre los cañaverales
los espíritus trabajan.
Ogún Badagrí en la sombra
afila su negra daga . . .
—Mañana tendrá el amito
la mejor de las corbatas—
Dessalines grita: ¡Sangre!
L'Overture ruge: ¡Venganza!
mientras remoto, escondido,
por la profunda maraña,
Macandal bate su gongo
en la torva noche haitiana.

Cuba—ñáñigo y bachata—
Haití—vodú y calabaza—
Puerto Rico—burundanga—

Antilla, vaho pastoso
de templa recién cuajada.
Trajín de ingenio cañero.
Baño turco de melaza.
Aristocracia de dril
donde la vida resbala
sobre frases de natilla
y suculentas metáforas.
Estilización de costas
a cargo de entecas palmas.
Idioma blando y chorreoso
—mamey, cacao, guanábana—.
En negrito y cocotero
Babbitt turista te atrapa;
Tartarín sensual te sueña
en tu loro y tu mulata;

It's voodoo. The power hour
of zombies and frogs.
Over the cane fields
spirits are at work.
Ogún Badagrí in shadow
hones his black knife . . .
—Tomorrow good ole Massa
wears the best of ties*—
Dessalines cries out: *Sang!*
L'Overture roars: *Venganze!*
while somewhere lurking
in kinky thicket,
Macandal beats his drum
in Haiti's fierce night.

Cuba—*ñáñigos* and good times—
Haiti—voodoo and gourds—
Puerto Rico—a hodgepodge—

Island, pastel odor
of cane juice distemper.
White linen aristocracy
where life glides
over custard phrases
and succulent metaphors.
Coasts outlined
in languid palm trees.
A bland, dripping language
—*mamey, cacao, guanábana.*
In darkie and coconut grove
Babbitt the tourist captures you,
fancying a sensual Tartary
from your parrot and mulatta;

*Rebel slaves would pull out the vicitim's tongue through the slit throat.

sólo a veces Don Quijote,
por chiflado y musaraña,
de tu maritornería
construye una dulcineada.

Cuba—ñáñigo y bachata—
Haití—vodú y calabaza—
Puerto Rico—burundanga—

only sometimes Don Quixote,
being daft and lost in fog,
from your Maritornes whoring
fabricates a Dulcinea.

Cuba—*ñáñigos* and good times—
Haití—voodoo and gourds—
Puerto Rico—a hodgepodge—

Ñáñigo al Cielo

El ñáñigo sube al cielo.
El cielo se ha decorado
de melón y calabaza
para la entrada del ñáñigo.
Los ángeles, vestidos
con verdes hojas de plátano,
lucen coronas de anana
y espadones de malango.
La gloria del Padre Eterno
rompe en triunfal taponazo,
y espumas de serafines
se riega por los espacios.
El ñáñigo va rompiendo
tiernas oleadas de blanco,
en su ascensión milagrosa
al dulce mundo seráfico.
Sobre el cerdo y caimán
Jehová, el potente, ha triunfado . . .
¡Gloria a Dios en las alturas
que nos trae por fin el ñáñigo!

Fiesta del cielo. Dulzura
de merengues y caratos,
mermelada de oraciones,
honesta horchata de salmos.
Con dedos de bronce y oro,
las trompas de los heraldos
por los balcones del cielo
cuelgan racimos de cantos.
Para aclararse la voz,
los querubes sonrosados
del egregio coro apuran
huevos de Espíritu Santo.
El buen humor celestial
hace alegre despilfarro

Ñáñigo to Heaven

The *ñáñigo* climbs to heaven.
Heaven is festooned
with melons and pumpkins,
for the *ñáñigo*'s entrance.
Robed in green plaintain fronds,
the angels sport
pineapple crowns
and tuber broadswords.
The Eternal Father's glory
erupts in triumphal uncorking
and a seraphim froth
spills throughout the cosmos.
The *ñáñigo* is breaking
mild waves of white
in his miraculous ascension
to the sweet seraphic world.
Jehovah the Powerful has prevailed
over the pig and the cayman . . .
Glory to God in the highest,
who finally brings us the *ñáñigo!*

Celestial feasting! Merengue
and custard-apple sweetness,
marmelade of prayers,
pure orgeat of psalm.
With bronze and gold fingers
the heralds's trumpets hang
along heaven's balconies
musical notes in bunches.
To clear their voices,
blushing cherubs
of the eminent choir
swallow Holy Spirit eggs.
The celestial good humor
has everyone guffawing

de chistes de muselina,
en palabras que ha lavado
de todo tizne terreno
el cielo azul de los santos.

El ñáñigo asciende por
la escalinata de mármol
con meneo contagioso
de caderas y omoplatos.
—Las órdenes celestiales
le acogen culipandeando—.

Hete aquí las blancas órdenes
del cermonial hierático:
La Orden del Golpe de Pecho,
la Orden del Ojo Extasiado,
la que preside San Memo
la Real Orden de San Mamo,
las parsimoniosas órdenes
del Arrojo Sacrosanto
que con matraca y rabel
barren el cielo de diablos.

En loa del alma nueva
que el Empíreo ha conquistado,
ondula el cielo en escuadras
de doctores y de santos.
Con arrobos maternales,
a que contemplen el ñáñigo
las castas once mil vírgenes
traen a los niños nonatos.
Las Altas Cancillerías
despliegan sus diplomáticos,
y se ven, en el desfile,
con eximio goce extático
y clueca sananería
de capones gallipavos.

at bedsheet jokes told
in words washed clean
of all terrestial filth
in the saints's bluing heaven.

Up the marble stairs
the *ñáñigo* ascends
contagiously shaking
hips and shoulder blades.
—Swaying their own asses,
heaven's Orders welcome him.

Here the white Orders
of the hieratic liturgy:
the Order of the Beat on the Chest,
the Order of the Entranced Eye,
the one presided over by San Memo,
the Royal Order of San Mamo,
the parsimonious Orders
of the Sacrosanct Audacity
whose rebeck and wooden rattle
sweep heaven of demons.

In honor of the new soul
the Empyrean has conquered
squadrons of church doctors and saints
cross the sky in waves.
Maternally driven,
the chaste eleven thousand virgins
gather their unborn
for a good look at the *ñáñigo*.
The High Chancilleries
unfurl their diplomats,
who bright-faced parade
their eminent ecstatic joy
and their Tom-capon's
clucking wholesomeness.

De pronto Jehová conmueve
de una patada el espacio.
Rueda el trueno y quedan solos
frente a frente, Dios y el ñáñigo.
—En la diestra del Señor,
agrio foete, fulge el rayo.

(Palabra de Dios, no es música
transportable a ritmo humano,
lo que Jehová preguntara,
lo que respondiera el ñáñigo,
pide un más noble instrumento
y exige un atril más alto.
Ataquen, pues, los exégetas
el tronco de tal milagro,
y quédese mi romance
por las ramas picoteando.
Pero donde el pico es corto,
vista y olfato van largos,
y mientras aquélla mira
a Dios y al negro abrazados,
éste percibe un mareante
tufo de ron antillano,
que envuelve las dos figuras
protagonistas del cuadro,
y da tonos de cumbancha
al festival del espacio).

¿Por qué va aprisa San Memo?
¿Por qué está alegre San Mamo?
¿Por qué las once mil vírgenes
sobre los varones castos
echan con grave descoco
la carga de los nonatos?
¿Quién enciende en las alturas
tan borococo antillano,

Suddenly Jehovah quakes
the cosmos with one step.
Thunder rolls and alone stand
God and *ñáñigo,* face to face.
—In the Lord's right hand,
a sharp whip cracks lightning.

(God's word isn't a music
human rhythms can interpret;
what Jehovah inquired,
what the *ñáñigo* answered,
begs a nobler instrument
and a higher music stand.
Cut down if you must, exegetes,
the trunk of such a miracle,
my romance still goes on
chirping in its branches.
But where beak proves short,
sight and smell reach farther,
and while the former sees
God and black man hugging,
the latter smells a dizzying
whiff of Caribbean rum
as it wraps around the scene's
two principal players,
layering a tone of jamboree
to the cosmic festivies.)

Why does San Memo hurry?
Why is San Mamo happy?
Why with brazen impudence
do the eleven thousand virgins
make the chaste men
babysit the unborn children?
Who inflames on high
such a Caribbean hearthrob

que en oleadas de bochinche
estremece los espacios?
¿Cuya es esa gran figura
que va dando barquinazos,
con su rezongo de truenos
y su orla azul de relámpagos?

Ha entrado un alma en el cielo
¡y ésa es el alma del ñáñigo!

that amid waves of gossip
rocks and rolls the cosmos?
Who's that giant figure
bumping and swaying
with his thunder-like growl
and framed in blue lightning?

A soul has entered heaven,
and that is the soul of the *ñáñigo!*

Numen

Jungla africana—Tembandumba.
Manigua haitiana—Macandal.

Al bravo ritmo del candombe
despierta el tótem ancestral:
pantera, antílope, elefante,
sierpe, hipopótamo, caimán.
En el silencio de la selva
bate el tambor sacramental,
y el negro baila poseído
de la gran bestia original.

Jungla africana—Tembandumba.
Manigua haitiana—Macandal.

Todo en atizo de fogatas,
bruja cazuela tropical,
cuece la noche mayombera
el negro embó de Obatalá.
Cuajos de sombra se derriten
sobre la llama roja y dan
en grillo y rana su sofrito
de ardida fauna nocturnal.

Jungla africana—Tembandumba.
Manigua haitiana—Macandal.

Es la Nigricia. Baila el negro.
Atravesando inmensidades
sobre el candombe su alma va
al limbo oscuro donde impera
la negra fórmula esencial.
Dale su fuerza el hipopótamo,
coraza bríndale el caimán,
le da sigilo la serpiente,

Numen

African jungle—Tembandumba.
Haitian thicket—Macandal.

Warrior candombe rhythms
arouse ancestral totems:
panther, antelope, elephant,
snake, hippo, crocodile.
In the jungle's silence,
sacramental drums
as blacks dance possessed
of the great primal beast.

African jungle—Tembandumba.
Haitian thicket—Macandal.

Engulfed in roaring fire,
like a tropic witch's pot
the Mayombe night brews
Obatalá's black magic.
Great gobs of shadow
melt over red flames,
infuse in cricket and frog,
their seared, night-fauna taste.

African jungle—Tembandumba.
Haitian thicket—Macandal.

It is Blackland. The black man dances.
Crossing vast reaches,
on the *candombe* his soul rides
to the dark limbo reign
of the first essence of black.
His strength's the hippo's gift,
his courage the crocodile's,
the snake lends stealth,

el antílope agilidad,
y elefante poderoso
rompiendo selvas al pasar,
le abre camino hacia el profundo
y eterno numen ancestral.

Jungla africana—Tembandumba.
Manigua haitian—Macandal.

the antelope speed,
and the overpowering elephant,
ploughing jungles with each step,
clears his path to the ultimate
and eternal ancestral numen.

African jungle—Tembandumba.
Haitian thicket—Macandal.

Pueblo Negro

Esta noche me obsede la remota
visión de un pueblo negro . . .
—Mussumba, Tombuctú, Farafangana—
es un pueblo de sueño,
tumbado allá en mis brumas interiores
a la sombra de claros cocoteros.

La luz rabiosa cae
en duros ocres sobre el campo extenso.
Humean, rojas de calor, las piedras,
y la humedad del árbol corpulento
evapora frescuras vegetales
en el agrio crisol del clima seco.

Pereza y laxitud. Los aguazales
cuajan un vaho amoniacal y denso.
El compacto hipopótamo se hunde
en su caldo de lodo suculento,
y el elefante de marfil y grasa
rumia bajo el baobab su vago sueño.

Allá entre las palmeras
está tendido el pueblo . . .
—Mussumba, Tombuctú, Farafangana—
caserío irreal de paz y sueño.

Alguien disuelve perezosamente
un canto monorrítmico en el viento,
pululado de úes que se aquietan
en balsas de diptongos soñolientos,
y de guturaciones alargadas
que dan un don de lejanía al verso.

Black Town

Tonight I keep seeing far-off
a vision of a black town . . .
—Mussumba, Timbucktu, Farafangana—
a dreamstuff town
cast out in my hazy soul,
in the shade of sunny coconut palms.

The raging light layers
hard ochre over vast land.
Red-hot, the stones sweat steam,
and the moisture of huge trees
mists to a plant coolness
in the acrid crucible of arid air.

Laziness and laxness. Stagnant pools
curd an ammonial, dense stench.
The compact hippo sinks
in its luscious mud broth,
and the fat and ivory elephant
chews its vague dream under the baobab.

Far-off among palm trees
the entire town is visible . . .
—Mussumba, Timbucktu, Farafangana—
unreal dwellings of peace and dream.

Someone lazily dissolves in the wind
refrained rhythms of a song
buzzing with u's becalmed
on rafts of dreamy dipthongs
and whose elastic gutturals
add a sense of distance to the lyrics.

Es la negra que canta
su sobria vida de animal doméstico;
la negra de las zonas soleadas
que huele a tierra, a salvajina, a sexo.
Es la negra que canta,
y su canto sensual se va extendiendo
como una clara atmósfera de dicha
bajo la sombra de los cocoteros.

Al rumor de su canto
todo se va extinguiendo,
y sólo queda en mi alma
la ú profunda del diptongo fiero,
en cuya curva maternal se esconde
la armonía prolífica del sexo.

It is the black woman singing
her simple life as a domestic animal;
the black woman from sunbaked zones,
who smells of earth, of game, of sex.
It is the black woman singing,
and her sensual song spreads
like a bright atmosphere of bliss
in the shade of coconut palms.

To her dying murmured song
everything slowly fades
until my soul only holds
the primal dipthong's deep u,
whose maternal curve secretes
the prolific harmony of sex.

Candombe

Los negros bailan, bailan, bailan,
ante la fogata encendida.
Tum-cutum, tum-cutum,
ante la fogata encendida.

Bajo el cocal, junto al oleaje,
dientes feroces de lascivia,
cuerpos de fango y de melaza,
senos colgantes, vaho de axilas,
y ojos de brillos tenebrosos
que el gongo profundo encandila.
Bailan los negros en la noche
ante la fogata encendida.
Tum-cutum, tum-cutum,
ante la fogata encendida.

¿Quién es el cacique más fuerte?
¿Cuál es la doncella más fina?
¿Dónde duerme el caimán más fiero?
¿Qué hechizo ha matado a Babissa?
Bailan los negros sudorosos
ante la fogata encendida.
Tum-cutum, tum-cutum,
en la soledad de la isla.

La luna es tortuga de plata
nadando en la noche tranquila.
¿Cuál será el pescador osado
que, a su red la traiga prendida:
Sokola, Babiro, Bombassa,
Yombofré, Bulón o Babissa?
Tum-cutum, tum-cutum,
ante la fogata encendida.

Candombe

Black men dance, dance, dance
round the roaring flames,
Tum-cutum, tum-cutum,
round the roaring flames.

Under coconuts, before ocean waves,
ferocious, lascivious teeth,
bodies coated with mud and molasses,
armpit smells, dangling breasts,
and coal-glazed eyes
the deep *gongo* ignites.
Black men dance at night
round the roaring flames,
Tum-cutum, tum cu-tum,
round the roaring flames.

Who is the bravest chief?
Which the loveliest maiden?
Where sleeps the meanest croc?
What spell killed Babissa?
Black men dance at night
round the roaring flames,
Tum-cutum, tum cu-tum,
in the island's solitude.

The moon is a silver tortoise
swimming in placid night.
Who'll be the fearless fisher
to bring it trapped in his net:
Sokola, Babiro, Bombassa,
Yombofré, Bulón or Babissa?
Tum-cutum, tum-cutum,
round the roaring flames.

Mirad la luna, el pez de plata,
la vieja tortuga maligna
echando al agua de la noche
su jugo que aduerme y hechiza . . .
Coged la luna, coged la luna,
traedla a un anzuelo prendida.
Bailan los negros en la noche
ante la fogata encendida.
Tum-cutum, tum-cutum,
ante la fogata encendida.

Tenemos el diente del dingo,
Gran Abuelo del Gran Babissa;
tenemos el diente del dingo
y una uña de lagartija . . .
contra todo mal ellos pueden,
de todo mal nos inmunizan.
Tenemos el diente del dingo
y una uña de lagartija.

Manasa, Cumbalo, Bilongo,
pescad esa luna podrida
que nos envenena la noche
con su hedionda luz amarilla.
Pescad la luna, pescad la luna,
el monstruo pálido que hechiza
nuestra caza y nuestras mujeres
en la soledad de la isla.
Tum-cutum, tum-cutum,
ante la fogata encendida.

Negros bravos de los palmares,
venid, que los espera Babissa
el Gran Rey del Caimán y el Coco,
ante la fogata encendida.
Tum-cutum, tum-cutum,
ante la fogata encendida.

Look, the moon, the silver fish,
the old evil tortoise
pissing into the night's water
its sedating, enchanting juice . . .
Catch the moon, catch the moon,
bring it dangling on a hook.
Black men dance at night
round the roaring flames,
Tum-cutum, tum-cutum,
round the roaring flames.

We have the dingo's tooth
Great Grandfather of the Great Babisso;
we have the dingo's tooth,
and a lizard's claw . . .
more powerful than any evil,
they armor us from all harm.
We have the dingo's tooth,
and a lizard's claw.

Manassa, Cumbalo, Bilongo,
fish that putrid moon
Poisoning our night
with its filthy yellow rays.
Fish the moon, fish the moon,
the pale monster that bewitches
our women and our game
in the island's solitude.
Tum-cutum, tum-cutum,
round the roaring flames.

Brave blacks of the palm groves,
come, awaiting is Babissa,
Great King of Cayman and Coconut,
round the roaring flames.
Tum-cutum, tum-cutum,
round the roaring flames.

Bombo

La bomba dice:—¡Tombuctú!
Cruzan las sombras ante el fuego.
Arde la pata de hipopótamo
en el balele de los negros.
Sobre la danza Bombo rueda
su ojo amarillo y soñoliento,
y el bembe de ídolo africano
le cae en cuajo sobre el pecho.
¡Bombo del Congo, mongo máximo,
Bombo del Congo está contento!

Allá en la jungla de mandinga
—Baobab, calaba y cocotero—
bajo el conjuro de los brujos
brota el terrible tótem negro,
mitad caimán y mitad sapo,
mitad gorila y mitad cerdo.
¡Bombo del Congo, mongo máximo,
Bombo del Congo está contento!

El es el numen fabuloso
cuyo poder no tiene término.
A su redor traza Nigricia
danzantes círculos guerreros.
Mongos, botucos y alimamis
ante Él se doblan en silencio,
y hasta el ju-jú de las cavernas
en tenebrosas magias diestro,
tiembla de miedo ante sus untos
cuando su voz truena en el trueno.
¡Bombo del Congo, mongo máximo,
Bombo del Congo está contento!

Bombo

The *bomba* says: "Timbuktu!"
Shadows crisscross before the fire.
Leg of hippo roasts
at the black tribe's feast.
Above the dance, Bombo rolls
his drowsy, yellow eyes
as his fat, African-idol lip
thickly sags over his chest.
Bombo of the Congo, highest chief,
Bombo of the Congo is now pleased.

Off in Mandingue jungle
—Baobabs, gourds, coconut grove—
the witchman's songs invoke
the powerful black totem,
half crocodile and half toad,
half gorilla and half hog.
Bombo of the Congo, highest chief,
Bombo of the Congo is now pleased.

He is the legendary numen
whose power nothing defines.
Around him Blackland orbits
warriors in circular dance.
Chiefs, sorcerers and witch doctors,
before Him respectfully bow
and even the cave-dwelling Juju,
skillful in black magic,
shudders in dread before his ointments
when His voice thunders in thunder.
Bombo of the Congo, highest chief,
Bombo of the Congo is now pleased.

¡Feliz quien bebe del pantano
donde Él sumerge su trasero!
Contra ése nada podrá el llanto
engañoso del caimán negro.
Bajo su maza formidable
todo rival caerá deshecho;
podrá dormirse en pleno bosque
a todo ruin cuidado ajeno,
y el hipopótamo y la luna
respetarán su grave sueño.

Venid, hermanos, al balele.
Bailad la danza del dios negro
alrededor de la fogata
donde arde el blanco prisionero.
Que la doncella más hermosa
rasgue su carne y abra el sexo,
para que pase, fecundándola,
el más viril de los guerreros.

Venid hermanos, al balele.
La selva entera está rugiendo.
Esta es la noche de mandinga
donde se forma un mundo nuevo.
Duerme el caimán, duerme la luna,
todo enemigo está durmiendo . . .
Somos los reyes de la tierra
que a Bombo, el dios, sólo tememos.

Venid, hermanos, al balele.
Crucen las sombras ante el fuego,
arda la pata de hipopótamo,
resuene el gongo en el silencio . . .
¡Bombo del Congo, mongo máximo,
Bombo del Congo está contento!

Happy is he who drinks from the swamp
where He dips His behind!
Before that one the black croc's
phoney tears are powerless.
Under his invincible mace
every enemy will be crushed;
deep in brush he can sleep
fearing no possible harm,
and neither hippo nor moon
dare disturb his soundest sleep.

Join, brothers, in the dance.
Dance the dance to the black god,
round and round the tall fire
that roasts the white captive.
Order the most beautiful maiden
to scar her flesh and open her sex,
so the most virile warrior
may plow and sow his seed.

Join, brothers, in the dance.
The entire jungle is roaring.
On this Mandingo night
a new world is born.
The crocodile sleeps, the moon sleeps,
our every enemy is sleeping . . .
Kings of the earth are we
who only fear the god Bombo.

Join, brothers, in the dance.
Crisscross shadows before the fire,
Roast the hippo leg,
Beat *gongos* in the silence . . .
Bombo of the Congo, highest chief,
Bombo of the Congo is now pleased.

Majestad Negra

Por la encendida calle antillana
va Tembandumba de la Quimbamba
—rumba, macumba, candombe, bámbula—
entre dos filas de negras caras.
Ante ella un congo—gongo y maraca—
ritma una conga bomba que bamba.

Culipandeando la reina avanza
y de su inmensa grupa resbalan
meneos cachondos que el gongo cuaja
en ríos de azúcar y de melaza.
Prieto trapiche de sensual zafra,
el caderamen, masa con masa,
exprime ritmos, suda que sangra,
y la molienda culmina en danza.

Por la encendida calle antillana
va Tembandumba de la Quimbamba.
Flor de Tórtola, rosa de Uganda,
por ti crepitan bombas y bámbulas;
por ti en calendas desenfrenadas
quema la Antilla su sangre ñáñiga.
Haití te ofrece sus calabazas;
fogosos rones te da jamaica;
Cuba te dice: ¡dale, mulata!
Y Puerto Rico: ¡melao, melamba!

¡Sus, mis cocolos de negras caras!
Tronad, tambores; vibrad, maracas.
Por la encendida calle antillana
—rumba, macumba, candombe, bámbula.—
va Tembandumba de la Quimbamba.

Black Majesty

Down the dance-hot Caribbean street,
shakes Tembandumba of the Quimbamba
—*rumba, macumba, candombe, bámbula*—
between two rows of black faces.
Leading her, a band—*gongos* and maracas—
pounds a catchy, ass-bouncing *conga.*

Curvaceous behind, the Queen advances
and from her huge rump slide
sexual jiggles that drums distill,
streaming as cane juice and molasses.
Black sugar mill for a sensual harvest,
her great thighs, mass against mass,
extract rhythms, sweating, bleeding,
so the grinding culminates in dance.

Down the dance-hot Caribbean street,
shakes Tembandumba of the Quimbamba.
Flower of Tortola, Rose of Uganda,
You ignite bombas and bámbulas;
You are why on wild moonless nights
the Island inflames its *ñáñigo* blood.
Haiti offers you its gourds;
scorching rums from Jamaica;
Cuba sings: Swing it, mulatta!
And Puerto Rico: Molasses! Oh, lick it!

Play on, my black-faced islanders!
Thunder, drums; rattle, maracas.
Down the dance-hot Caribbean street,
—*rumba, macumba, candombe, bámbula*—
shakes Tembandumba of the Quimbamba.

Danza Negra

Calabó y bambú.
Bambú y calabó.
El Gran Cocoroco dice: tu-cu-tu.
La Gran Cocoroca dice: to-co-to.
Es el sol de hierro que arde en Tombuktú.
Es la danza negra de Fernando Poo.
El cerdo en el fango gruñe: pru-pru-pru.
El sapo en la charca sueña: cro-cro-cro.
Calabó y bambú.
Bambú y calabó.

Rompen los junjunes en furiosa ú.
Los gongos trepidan con profunda ó
Es la raza negra que ondulando va
en el ritmo gordo del mariyandá.
Llegan los botucos a la fiesta ya.
Danza que te danza la negra se da.

Calabó y bambú.
Bambú y calabó.
El Gran Cocoroco dice: tu-cu-tu.
La Gran Cocoroca dice: to-co-to.

Pasan tierras rojas, islas de betún:
Haití, Martinica, Congo, Camerún;
las papamientosas antillas del ron
y las patualesas islas del volcán,
que en el grave son
del canto se dan.

Black Dance

Black wood and bamboo.
Bamboo and black wood.
The He-Muckamuck sings: too-coo-too.
The She-Muckamuck sings: toe-co-toe.
It's the branding-iron sun's burn in Timbuktu.
It's the black dance danced on Fernando Po.*
The mud-fest hog grunts: pru-pru-pru.
The bog-wet toad dreams: cro-cro-cro.
Black wood and bamboo.
Bamboo and black wood.

Juju strings strum a tempest of oos.
Tomtoms throb with dark bass ohs.
It's wave on wave of the black race in
the bloated rhythm of *mariyandá.*
Chieftains join the feasting now.
The Negress dances, dances entranced.
Black wood and bamboo.
Bamboo and black wood.
The He-Muckamuck sings: too-coo-too.
The She-Muckamuck sings: toe-co-toe.

Red lands pass, bootblack islands:
Haiti, Martinique, Congo, Cameroon;
the *papiamiento* Antilles of rum,
the volcano's patois isles,
in rythmic abandon
to dark-voweled song.

*Situated off the Western African coast, this island was famous for its slave mills.

Calabó y bambú.
Bambú y calabó.
Es el sol de hierro que arde en Tombuktú.
Es la danza negra de Fernando Poo.
Es el alma africana que vibrando está
en el ritmo gordo del mariyandá.

Calabó y bambú.
Bambú y calabó.
El Gran Cocoroco dice: tu-cu-tu.
La Gran Cocoroca dice: to-co-to.

Black wood and bamboo.
Bamboo and black wood.
It's the branding-iron sun's burn in Timbuktu.
It's the black dance danced on Fernando Po.
It's the African soul that is throbbing in
the bloated rhythm of *mariyandá.*

Black wood and bamboo.
Bamboo and black wood.
The He-Muckamuck sings: too-coo-too.
The She-Muckamuck sings: toe-co-toe.

Kalahari

¿Por qué ahora la palabra Kalahari?

El día es hermoso y claro. En la luz bailotean
con ágil gracia, seres luminosos y alegres:
el pájaro, la brizna de hierba, las cantáridas,
y las moscas que en vuelo redondo y embriagado
rebotan contra el limpio cristal de mi ventana.
A veces una nube blanca lo llena todo
con su mole rolliza, hinchada, bombonosa,
y es como un imponente pavo real del cielo.

¿Por qué ahora la palabra Kalahari?

Anoche estuve de francachela con los amigos,
y derivamos hacia un lupanar absurdo
allá por el sombrío distrito de los muelles . . .
El agua tenebrosa ponía un vaho crudo
de marisco, y el viento ondulaba premioso
a través de los tufos peculiares del puerto.
En el burdel reían estrepitosamente
las mujeres de bocas pintadas . . . Sin embargo,
una, inmóvil, callaba; callaba sonreída,
y se dejaba hacer sonreída y callada.
Estaba ebria. Las cosas sucedían distantes.
Recuerdo que alguien dijo—Camella, un trago, un trago.

¿Por qué ahora la palabra Kalahari?

Esta mañana, hojeando un magazín de cromos,
ante un perrillo de aguas con cinta roja al cuello,
estuve largo tiempo observando observando . . .
No sé por qué mi pensamiento a la deriva
fondeó en una bahía de claros cocoteros,
con monos, centenares de monos que trenzaban
una desordenada cadena de cabriolas.

Kalahari

Why now the word Kalahari?

Perfect the bright day. In sunlight, with nimble grace,
flicker lively, glossy creations:
birds, blades of grass, blister beetles,
and flies whose circular, drunk paths
crash into my window's clean pane.
Sometimes it's all white with one cloud's,
rolling, swollen, puffy mass,
an august peacock of the sky.

Why now the word Kalahari?

Last night I barhopped with friends
until we came to an absurd brothel
over by the shadowy wharf . . .
Black water oozed a raw stench
of shellfish, and the wind blew slowly
across the port's strong odors.
In the brothel, red-lipped women
laughed raucously . . . But among them
one, motionless, kept quiet; smilingly quiet,
letting herself be felt up, smiling and quiet.
She was drunk. Everything happened far away.
I remember someone's saying, "Camel, a drink, a drink."

Why now the word Kalahari?

This morning as I browsed a magazine's color photos
a spaniel puppy with red ribbon collar
held my attention, held it for a long time.
Don't know why, but my thoughts adrift
cast anchor at a bay of sunny palm trees
with monkeys, monkeys by the hundreds
braiding a riotous chain of leaps.

¿Por qué ahora la palabra Kalahari?

Ha surgido de pronto, inexplicablemente . . .
¡Kalahari! ¡Kalahari! ¡Kalahari!
¿De dónde habrá surgido esta palabra
escondida como un insecto en mi memoria;
picada como una mariposa disecada
en la caja de coleópteros de mi memoria,
y ahora viva, insistiendo revoloteando ciega
contra la luz ofuscadora del recuerdo?
¡Kalahari! ¡Kalahari! ¡Kalahari!

¿Por qué ahora la palabra Kalahari?

Why now the word Kalahari?

It has emerged suddenly, inexplicably. . .
Kalahari! Kalahari! Kalahari!
Emerged from where, this word
hidden like an insect in my memory,
pinned like a desiccated butterfly
in my beetle-box memory
and now alive, persistent, fluttering blind
against recall's distorting light?
Kalahari! Kalahari! Kalahari!

Why now the word Kalahari?

Elegía del Duque de la Mermelada

¡Oh mi fino, mi melado Duque de la Mermelada!
¿Dónde están tus caimanes en el lejano aduar del Pongo,
y la sombra azul y redonda de tus baobabs africanos,
y tus quince mujeres olorosas a selva y a fango?

Ya no comerás el suculento asado de niño,
ni el mono familiar, a la siesta, te matará los piojos,
ni tu ojo dulce rastreará el paso de la jirafa afeminada
a través del silencio plano y caliente de las sabanas.

Se acabaron tus noches con su suelta cabellera de fogatas
y su gotear soñoliento y perenne de tamboriles,
en cuyo fondo te ibas hundiendo como un lodo tibio
hasta llegar a las márgenes últimas de tu gran bisabuelo.

Ahora, en el molde vistoso de tu casaca francesa,
pasas azucarado de saludos como un cortesano cualquiera,
a despecho de tus pies que desde sus botas ducales
te gritan: —Babilongo, súbete por las cornisas del palacio

¡Qué gentil va mi Duque con la Madama de Cafolé,
todo afelpado y pulcro en la onda azul de los violines,
conteniendo las manos que desde sus guantes de aristócrata
le gritan: —Babilongo, derríbala sobre ese capané de rosa!

Desde las márgenes últimas de tu gran bisabuelo,
a través del silencio plano y caliente de las sabanas,
¿por qué lloran tus caimanes en el lejano aduar del Pongo,
¡oh mi fino, mi melado Duque de la Mermelada!?

Elegy on the Duke of Marmalade

Oh my fine, my honey-colored Duke of Marmalade!
Where are your crocodiles in the far-off village on the Pongo,
and the round blue shadow of your African baobabs,
and your fifteen wives smelling of mud and jungle?

No longer will you eat the succulent roast child,
nor will the family monkey kill your lice at siesta,
nor your fond eye trail the effeminate giraffe
across the hot flat silence of the plains.

Gone your nights with their flowing hair of bonfire
and their lulling, ceaseless dripping of drums,
into whose depths you'd sink slowly as into warm mud
to the farthest shores of your great great-grandfather.

Now in the loud design of your French dress-coat,
you parade, candied by greetings like any courtier,
despite your feet that from their ducal boots
cry out to you: "Babilongo, climb up to the cornices of the palace."

How genteel goes my Duke with Madame de Cafaulait,
all velvet and refinement on the violins' blue wave,
holding back his hands that, gloved like an aristocrat's,
cry out to him: "Babilongo, knock her down on the rose settee."

From the farthest shores of your great great-grandfather,
across the hot flat silence of the plains,
why do your crocodiles weep in the far-off village on the Pongo,
Oh my fine, my honey-colored Duke of Marmalade?

Ten con Ten

Estás, en pirata y negro,
mi isla verde estilizada,
el negro te da la sombra,
te da la línea el pirata.
Tambor y arcabuz a un tiempo
tu morena gloria exaltan,
con rojas flores de pólvora
y bravos ritmos de bámbula.

Cuando el huracán desdobla
su fiero acordeón de ráfagas,
en la punta de los pies
—ágil bayadera—danzas
sobre la alfombra del mar
con fina pierna de palmas.

Podrías ir de mantilla,
si tu ardiente sangre ñáñiga
no trocara por madrás
la leve espuma de España.

Podrías lucir, esbelta,
sobriedad de línea clásica,
si tu sol, a fuerza de oro,
no madurase tus ánforas
dilatando sus contornos
en amplitud de tinaja.

Pasarías ante el mundo
por civil y ciudadana,
si tu axila—flor de sombra—
no difundiera en las plazas
el rugiente cebollín
que sofríen tus entrañas.

Not This, Not That

You are, my green island,
sketched in pirate and black,
blacks fill in the shading
pirates the outline.
Drum and harquebus at once
extol your dark beauty,
with red gunpowder flowers
and wild rhythmic *bámbula.*

When the hurricane pumps
its fierce accordion of gusts,
on the tips of your toes,
you—graceful bayadere—
with slender palm-tree legs
dance on the carpet sea.

You could have strolled in mantilla,
if your hot *ñáñigo* blood
hadn't bartered for madras
the light linen of Spain.

You could've shone, shapely,
sobriety in a classic mold,
if your sun's strong gold
hadn't ripened your amphora thighs
expanding their form
wide as water jars.

You would've passed before the world
for cultured and civilized,
if your armpits—shadow flowers—
didn't spread in the plazas
the pungent oniony odor
your insides sautée.

Y así estás, mi verde antilla,
en un sí es que no es de raza,
en ten con ten de abolengo
que te hace tan antillana . . .
Al ritmo de los tambores
tu lindo ten con ten bailas,
una mitad española
y otra mitad africana.

So this, my green island, is you
an are too, am not over race
a not this, not that your pedigree
that makes you so Caribbean . . .
To drum rhythms you dance
your pretty not this, not that,
half of you Spanish,
the other African.

El Gallo

Un botonazo de luz,
luz amarilla, luz roja.
En la contienda, disparo
de plumas luminosas.
Energía engalanada
de la cresta a la cola
—ámbar, oro, terciopelo—
lujo que se deshoja
con heroico silencio
en la gallera estentórea.
Rueda de luz trazada
ante la clueca remolona,
la capa del ala abierta
y tendida en ronda . . .

Gallo, gallo del trópico.
Pico que destila auroras.
Relámpago congelado.
Paleta luminosa.
¡Ron de plumas que bebe
la Antilla brava y tórrida!

The Gamecock

A foil-thrust of light,
yellow light, red light.
In the fight, a shot
of radiant feathers.
Energy decked out
from crest to tail
—amber, gold, velvet—
opulence that molts
heroicly silent
in shout-filled arenas.
Luminous wheel traced
round the clucking hen,
open his plume cape
cloakingly stretched . . .

Rooster, cock of the tropics.
Beak distillary of dawns.
Congealed lightning bolt.
Dazzling palatte.
Plumed rum to quench
the sweltering Island defiant!

de *Intermedios del Hombre Blanco*

Islas

Las tierras del patois y el papiamento.
Acordeón con sordina de palmeras.
Azul profundidad de mar y cielo,
donde las islas quedan más aisladas.

Acordeón en la tarde.
Fluir perenne en soledad sin cauce.
Horizontal disolución de ideas,
en la melaza de los cantos negros.

Emoción de vacío,
con el trapiche abandonado al fondo,
y el cocolo bogando en su cachimbo
quién sabe hacia qué vago fondeadero.

Y en la terraza del hotel sin nombre,
algún aislado capacete blanco,
alelado de islas
bajo el puño de hierro de los rones.

from *White Man's Interludes*

Islands

Lands of patois and *papiamento.*
Accordion with palm trees mute.
Blue fathoms of sea and sky
isolating islands even more.

Accordion in the afternoon.
Perennial drift on a courseless solitude.
Ideas horizontally dissolving
in a molasses of black chant.

Atmosphere of emptiness:
a sugar mill abandoned in the background
and a black islander rowing his boat
who knows to what vague haven.

And on the terrace of the no-name hotel,
some enisled white pith helmet
drunk after too many islands
under the iron fist of rum.

de *Intermedios del Hombre Blanco*

Tambores

La noche es un criadero de tambores
que croan en la selva,
con sus roncas gargantas de pellejo
cuando alguna fogata los despierta.

En el lodo compacto de la sombra
parpadeado de ojillos de luciérnagas,
esos ventrudos bichos musicales
con sus patas de ritmo chapotean.

Con soñoliento gesto de batracios
alzan pesadamente la cabeza,
dando al cálido viento la pringosa
gracia de su energía tuntuneca.

Los oye el hombre blanco
perdido allá en las selvas . . .
Es un tuntún asiduo que se vierte
imponderable por la noche inmensa.

A su conjuro hierven
las oscuras potencias:
fetiches de la danza,
tótemes de la guerra,
y los mil y un demonios que pululan
por el cielo sensual del alma negra.

from *White Man's Interludes*

Drums

Night is a nursery of drums
whose hoarse, hide throats
croak in the jungle
when awakened by a bonfire.

In the packed-mud dark
blinking firefly eyes,
those paunchy musical reptiles
paddle their rhythm feet.

Drowsy as an amphibian looks
heavily they raise their heads,
lending the warm wind the larded
grace of their tomtom energy.

Hearing them is the white man
lost out in jungle . . .
A constant downpour of tomtoms
beyond words in the vast night.

Conjured by them,
the dark powers seethe:
fetishes for the dance,
totems for war,
and the thousand and one demons that teem
in the black soul's sensual heaven.

¡Ahí vienen los tambores!
Ten cuidado, hombre blanco, que a ti llegan
para clavarte su aguijón de música.
Tápate las orejas,
cierra toda abertura de tu alma
y el instinto dispón a la defensa;
que si en la torva noche de Nigricia
te picara un tambor de danza o guerra,
su terrible ponzoña
correrá para siempre por tus venas.

Here come the drums!
Watch out, white man, they're coming to nail
their musical stingers in you.
Cover your ears,
close every pore in your soul
and prime your instinct to defend;
for if, in Blackland's angry night,
a war or dance drum stings you,
its potent venom
will course your veins forever.

Mulata-Antilla

En ti ahora, mulata,
me acojo al tibio mar de las Antillas.
Agua sensual y lenta de melaza,
puerto de azúcar, cálida bahía,
con la luz en reposo
dorando la onda limpia,
y en el soñoliento zumbo de colmena
que cuajan los trajines de la orilla.

En ti ahora, mulata,
cruzo el mar de las islas.
Eléctricos mininos de ciclones
en tus curvas se alargan y se ovillan,
mientras sobre mi barca va cayendo
la noche de tus ojos, pensativa.

En ti ahora, mulata . . .
¡oh despertar glorioso en las Antillas!
bravo color que el do de pecho alcanza,
música al rojo vivo de alegría,
y calientes cantáridas de aroma
—limón, tabaco, piña—
zumbando a los sentidos
sus embriagadas voces de delicia.

Eres ahora, mulata,
todo el mar y la tierra de mis islas.
Sinfonía frutal cuyas escalas
rompen furiosamente en tu catinga.
He aquí en su verde traje la guanábana
con sus finas y blandas pantaletas
de muselina; he aquí el caimito
con su leche infantil; he aquí la piña

Mulatta-Antille

In you, mulatta, I now embrace
the lukewarm sea of the Antilles.
A sensual, molasses-slow water,
a sugar-cane port, a warm bay
with a sunlight stopped to rest,
gilding cleanly-sculpted waves,
and in the lulling, beehive buzz
churned by the restless shore.

In you, mulatta, I now cross
the sea of many islands.
Electric feline cyclones
stretch and curl up in your curves,
as onto my boat slowly falls
the night of your eyes, deep in thought.

Now in you, mulatta, . . .
Oh glorious awakening on the Antilles!
Intense hue attained in a tenor's *do,*
music at revelry's red-hot tip,
and hot blister beetles of smells
—lemon, tobacco, pineapple—
drilling into the senses
their drunken chorus of delight.

Now you are, mulatta,
all my islands's landmass and surrounding sea.
Fruit symphony whose scales
overture furioso in your sweat.
Here in a green dress the soursop
with its fine, soft muslin bloomers;
here, the *caimito* with its
wetnurse milk; here the pineapple

con su corona de soprano. . . Todos
los frutos ¡oh mulata! tú me brindas,
en la clara bahía de tu cuerpo
por los soles del trópico bruñida.

Imperio tuyo, el plátano y el coco,
que apuntan su dorada artillería
al barco transeúnte que nos deja
su rubio contrabando de turistas.
En potro de huracán pasas cantando
tu criolla canción, prieta walkiria,
con centelleante espuela de relámpagos
rumbo al verde Walhalla de las islas.

Eres inmensidad libre y sin límites,
eres amor sin trabas y sin prisas;
en tu vientre conjugan mis dos razas
sus vitales potencias expansivas.
Amor, tórrido amor de la mulata,
gallo de ron, azúcar derretida,
tabonuco que el tuétano te abrasa
con aromas de sándalo y de mirra.
Con voces del Cantar de los Cantares,
eres morena porque el sol te mira.
Debajo de tu lengua hay miel y leche
y ungüento derramado en tus pupilas.
Como la torre de David, tu cuello,
y tus pechos gemelas cervatillas.
Flor de Sarón y lirio de los valles,
yegua de Faraón, ¡oh Sulamita!

Cuba, Santo Domingo, Puerto Rico,
fogosas y sensuales tierras mías.
¡Oh los rones calientes de Jamaica!
¡Oh fiero calalú de Martinica!
¡Oh noche fermentada de tambores
del Haití impenetrable y voduista!

crowned like a soprano . . . Every fruit,
oh mulatta, you offer me,
in that luminous bay your body
burnished by tropic suns.

Empire all yours, of plantain and coconut,
aiming their golden artillery
at what cruising ship leaves us
its blond contraband of tourists.
On a hurricane colt you ride by singing
your Creole song, dark Valkyrie,
flashing spurs of lightning
toward the green Valhalla of the islands.

You are open, boundless horizon
you are unfettered, unhurried love;
in your womb my two races conjugate
each's essential, generous force.
Love, torrid love of the mulatta,
wineskin of rum, warm caramel,
hardwood your marrow burns
fragrant with sandalwood and myhrr.
The Song of Songs turned to flesh,
dark is your skin because the sun ogles you.
Under your tongue, milk and honey,
and an ointment poured into your eyes.
Like the tower of David, your neck,
and twin fawns your breasts.
Rose of Sharon and Lily of the Valley,
Pharaoh's mare, Oh Salomé!

Cuba, Santo Domingo, Puerto Rico,
my fiery, sensual lands.

Oh scorching Jamaican rums!
Oh raw Martinican callaloo!
Oh night fermented from Haiti's
impenetrable voodoo drums!

Dominica, Tórtola, Guadalupe,
¡Antillas, mis Antillas!
Sobre el mar de Colón, aupadas todas,
sobre el Caribe mar, todas unidas,
soñando y padeciendo y forcejeando
contra pestes, ciclones y codicias,
y muriéndose un poco por la noche,
y otra vez a la aurora, redivivas,
porque eres tú, mulata de los trópicos,
la libertad cantando en mis Antillas.

Dominica, Tórtola, Guadalupe,
Antilles, my Antilles!
Over Columbus's sea, each reaching higher,
Over the Caribbean sea, all as one,
dreaming and suffering and striving
against plagues, hurricanes and crime,
and dying a little at night,
and reborn again at sunrise,
because you are, mulatta of the tropics,
Liberty in song in my Antilles!

Part III

1938-1944

Menú

Mi restorán abierto en el camino
para ti, trashumante peregrino.
Comida limpia y varia
sin truco de especiosa culinaria.

Hete aquí este paisaje digestivo
recién pescado en linfas antillanas:
rabo de costa en caldo de mar vivo,
con pimienta de luz y miel de ananas.

Si la inocua legumbre puritana
tu sobrio gusto siente,
y a su térreo sabor híncale el diente
tu simple propensión vegetariana,
aquí está este racimo de bohíos
que a hombro de monte acogedor reposa
—monte con barba jíbara de ríos,
de camarón y guábara piojosa—
sobre cuyas techumbres cae, espesa,
yema de sol batida en mayonesa.

Tengo, para los gustos ultrafinos,
platos que son la gloria de la mesa . . .
aquí están unos pinos,
pinos a la francesa
en verleniana salsa de crepúsculo.
(El chef Rubén, cuyos soberbios flanes
delicia son de líricos gurmanes,
les dedicó un opúsculo).

Si a lo francés prefieres lo criollo,
y tu apetencia, con loable intento,

Menu

My roadside restaurant is open
for you, pasture-seeking pilgrim.
Clean and varied food
artful not in spiced-up cookery.

Observe this digestive landscape
freshly fished in Caribbean waters:
coastal tail in broth of live sea,
with sunlight pepper and pineapple honey.

If what your sober relish craves
is the innocuous, Puritan legume
as your plain vegeterian bent
chomps for such earthy flavor,
try these clustered huts asleep
on a friendly mountain's shoulder
—mountain with rustic beard
of rivulets, shrimp, lice-sized crab—
huts on whose roofs thickly lays
a whipped, sun-yoke mayonnaise.

I have, for ultrarefined tastes,
dishes the splendor of any table . . .
here a serving of pines,
pines a la Francaise
in a Verlainian nightfall sauce.
(Chef Rubén,* whose superb flans
delight poetry's gourmands,
wrote them an opuscule.)

If over French you'd rather Creole,
and your palate, commendably inclined,

---

*Nicaraguan poet Rubén Darío (1867-1916) was the leading figure of modernismo, which emulated the French symbolists and emphasized a perfection of form.

pírrase por ajiaco y ajopollo
y sopón de embrujado condimento,
toma este calalú maravilloso
con que la noche tropical aduna
su maíz estrellado y luminoso,
y el diente de ajo de su media luna
en divino potaje sustancioso.

(Sopa de Martinica, caldo fiero
que el volcán Mont Peleé cuece y engorda;
los huracanes soplan el brasero,
y el caldo hierve, y sube, y se desborda,
en rebullente espuma de luceros).

Mas si en la gama vegetal persiste
tu aleccionado instinto pacifista,
con el vate de Asís, alado y triste,
y Gandhi, el comeyerbas teosofista,
tengo setas de nubes remojadas
en su entrañable exudación de orvallo,
grandes setas cargadas
con vitamina eléctrica de rayo,
que dan a quien su tónico acumula
la elemental potencia de la mula.

La casa luce habilidad maestra
creando inusitadas maravillas
de cosas naturales y sencillas,
para la lengua culturada y diestra.
Aquí te va una muestra:
palmeras al ciclón de las Antillas,
cañaveral horneado a fuego lento,
soufflé de platanales sobre el viento,
piñón de flamboyanes en su tinta,

kills for hot sauce, seasoned chicken,
and bewitched condiments in soup,
sample this enchanting callaloo,
in which the tropic night blends
its shining, corn-grain stars
and a garlic-clove half moon
in a divine, full-bodied stew.

(Martinican soup, potent broth
the volcano Mont Peleé simmers and swells;
hurricanes fan the coals,
so the broth simmers, rises, boils over
in a rumbling, many-eyed froth).

But if your disciplined pacifist impulse
must sustain a vegetarian note,
à la Assisi's winged, sad bard,
and Gandhi, theosophist grass eater,
I have cloud mushrooms soaked
in their slowly sweated juice,
huge mushrooms voltage-charged
with lightning-vitamins whose tonic
endows who takes them as a rule
the primal potency of a mule.

The house flaunts its premier talent,
creating from basic, natural things
singular marvels to please
the most skilled, cultivated tongue.
Here I submit a sample:
palm trees tossed in Caribbean cyclone,
cane fields broiled under slow flame,
souffle of windblown plantain grove,
a pie of flamboyants in their ink . . .

o merienda playera
de uveros y manglares en salmuera,
para dejar la gula regulada
al propio Saladín de la Ensalada.
Mi restorán te brinda sus servicios.
Arrímate a la mesa, pasajero,
come hasta hartar y séante propicios
los dioses de la Uva y el Puchero.

or a beach-outing snack
of pickled sea grapes and mangroves
to regulate the gluttony
of the very Saladin of Salad.
My restaurant offers you its service.
Approach the table, traveler,
eat your fill until you've honored
the gods of the Grape and Our Daily Bread.

Aires Bucaneros

para Jaime Benítez

Para el bucanero carne bucanada,
el largo mosquete de pólvora negra,
la roja camisa, la rústica abarca
y el tórrido ponche de ron con pimienta.

I

¡Ay, batatales de la Tortuga,
cacao en jícara de Nueva Reyna!
¡Huy, los caimanes de Maracaibo,
vómito prieto de Cartagena!

¡Ay, naranjales de La Española,
cazabe tierno de Venezuela!
¡Huy, tiburones de Portobelo,
berbén violáceo de la Cruz Vera!

II

Al bucanero densos perfumes,
el crudo aroma, la brava especia:
las bergamotas y los jenjibres,
los azafranes y las canelas.

¡Ay, blando chumbo de la criolla,
de la mulata tibia mameya!
¡Huy, la guanábana cimarrona
que abre su bruja flor en la negra!

¡Ay, duros ojos de la cautiva
que al bucanero locura llevan;
ojos que en su alma ya desataron
el zas fulmíneo de la centella!

Buccaneer Winds

for Jaime Benítez

Give the buccaneer *boucan* meat,
his long, black-powder musket,
his red shirt, his rawhide sandals,
and his scalding, peppered rum punch.

I

Ay, the yam fields of Tortuga,
cacao-filled gourds of New Spain!
Huy, the caymans of Maracaibo,
the yellow fever of Cartagena!

Ay, the orange groves of Hispaniola,
the green casava of Venezuela!
Huy, the sharks of Portobelo,
the purple scurvy of Vera Cruz!

II

Give the buccaneer potent perfumes,
abrasive aromas, jolting spices:
cinnamons and gingers,
saffrons and snuffs.

Ay, the white woman's soft cactus pears,
the mulatta's warm mammee fruit!
Huy, the wild soursop's witch flower
that blooms in the black woman.

Ay, the captive woman's hard eyes
drive the buccaneer mad;
eyes that into his soul already fired
the explosive shot of her wrath!

Mejor el ponche de moscabada,
mejor la pipa que al viento humea,
mejor el largo fusil de chispa,
mejor el torvo mastín de presa.

III

Al bucanero la res salvaje:
toro montuno, vaca mañera.
Las hecatombes en la manigua
al fulgor vivo de las hogueras.

¡Ay, el ternero desjarretado
que se asa al humo de fronda tierna!
Boucán en lonja para el almuerzo,
Toute chaude de tuétano para la cena.

¡Huy, fiera caña de las Antillas
que en viejo roble su diablo acendra,
y en las entrañas del bucanero,
agua del infierno, ruge violenta!

IV

Al bucanero las tierras vírgenes,
el agua indómita, la mar inédita;
los horizontes en donde aúlla
la agria jauría de la tormenta.

¡Ay, las maniguas paticerradas,
jaguar taimado, víbora artera!
¡Huy, tremedales de falso adorno,
árbol carnívoro, liana tremenda!

Better his molasses-laced rum,
better his wind-fogging pipe,
better his flashing long musket,
better his fierce hunting dog.

III

Give the buccaneer wilderness cattle:
rustic bulls, subtle cows.
The hundred jungle slaughters
by luminous, crackling pyres.

Ay, the ham-hacked veal
smoke-cured under young fronds!
Boucan strips for lunch;
Toute chaude marrow for dinner.

Huy, bestial Caribbean sugar cane
that refines in old oak its devil
and, in buccaneer's bowels
a hell water, roar with rage!

IV

Give the buccaneer virgin lands,
ungoverned waters, uncharted sea;
the horizon housing the howl
of a gnarling dog-pack storm.

Ay, the closed-thigh jungle,
the cunning jaguar, the crafty viper!
Huy, the marshes's deceptive adornments,
carnivorous trees, giant lianas!

¡Ay, letal sombra del manzanillo,
roja calina de las praderas,
miasmas envolventes de los manglares,
jején palúdico de las ciénagas!

Y en el delirio febricitante
voces fantasmas cruzan la selva . . .
¡Camalofote del camalote,
Bucaramángara la bucanera!

V

Al bucanero curvo machete,
puñal certero, pistola alerta;
ánima firme para el asalto
cuando columbra la esquiva presa.

¡Ay, galeón pavo que infla en el viento
su linajudo plumón de velas,
y, tenso el moco del contrafoque
-señor del agua-se pavonea!

Síguelo el lugre filibustero
en ominosas bordadas fieras:
gallo encastado del Mar Caribe,
el cuello al rape, limpia la espuela . . .

Y en la pelmele del abordaje
que funde el rezo con la blasfemia,
desmocha al pavo galeón del Golfo
la rubia traba filibustera.

Ay, the manchineel's poison shade,
the red fog of the meadows,
the mangrove's choking miasma,
the swamp's malarial mosquito!

And in feverous delusions
phantasmal voices haunt the thicket . . .
Camalofote of the water reeds,
Bucaramángara, the she-buccaneer!

V

Give the buccaneer a curved machete,
an accurate dagger, a loaded pistol;
his animus steeled for the attack
when he sights the elusive prey.

Ay, galleon turkey that in wind inflates
its pedigreed plumage of sails
and, tense its forehead-crest jib
—a seafaring gentleman—struts proud!

Chasing it, the freebooter's lugger
in ominous, fearless tacks:
the Caribbean's bred gamecock,
neck plucked, spurs sharp . . .

And in the helter-skelter boarding
that alloys prayer and profanity,
the blond filibustering hobble
beheads the Gulf's galleon turkey.

VI

Por el camino de Tierra Firme
campanilleando viene la recua.
Cincuenta mulas venezolanas
traen el tesoro de las Américas.

(Polvos auríferos de la montaña.
finas vicuñas de la meseta,
tórridas mieles de la llanura,
resinas mágicas de la selva).

Bosques y ríos, mares y montes,
sobre las mulas su carga vuelcan . . .
Oro idolátrico del Grande Inca,
Plata litúrgica del Noble Azteca.

La guardia altiva de los virreyes
cubre los flancos y al fondo cierra.
¡Ay, caravana que se confía
a la española lanza guerrera!

Contra ella irrumpen los bucaneros
machete al aire, bala certera,
y el botín pasa del león hispano
al tigre astuto de las Américas.

ᘏ ᘏ ᘏ

¡Tortuga! Puerto de la Cayona.
D'Ogeron rige, Le Grand acecha,
Levasseur lucha con Pedro Sangre
y Morgan trama su obra maestra.

VI

Along the continental road
parades the bell-tinkling drove.
Fifty Venezuelan mules
haul away the Americas's treasure.

(Mountain-mined gold dust,
fine high-plains vicuñas,
bracing flatland honeys,
magic jungle resins.)

Woodlands, rivers, seas, mountains,
unload their burden on muleback . . .
The Great Incas's idolatrous gold,
The Noble Aztecs's liturgical silver.

The Viceroy's arrogant guards
cover the flanks, close the rear.
Ay, caravan in the hands
of Spanish military lancers!

Against it storm the buccaneers,
machetes slashing, bullets exact,
as the Spanish lion's booty passes
to the Americas's shrewed tiger.

∾   ∾   ∾

Tortuga! Port La Cayona.
D'Ogeron rules, Le Grand lays in ambush,
Levasseur clashes with Peter Blood
and Morgan schemes his master plan.

En la posada del Rey Felipe
el dado corre y el naipe vuela,
mientras las bolsas en pugna lanzan
áureos relámpagos de monedas.

Noche de orgía, la hez del mundo
bulle en el fondo de las tabernas,
entre el repique de los doblones
y el tiquitoque de las botellas.

El vaho íntimo de las mujeres
prende en la sangre moscas de menta,
y a veces rompen contra el tumulto
los cataplunes de la refriega.

¡Ay, la Cayona del bucanero!
Ron y tabaco, puta y pelea,
juego de turba patibularia
que al diablo invoca por veinte lenguas.

Y cuando izada sobre Tortuga
—pendón corsario-la noche ondea,
la luna, cómplice de los piratas
fija en las sombras su calavera.

ॐ ॐ ॐ

Para el bucanero carne bucanada,
el largo mosquete de pólvora negra,
la roja camisa, la rústica abarca
y el tórrido ponche de ron con pimienta.

In King Phillip's Inn,
dice roll and playing cards fly,
as battling purses flash
gold-coin lightning.

Orgy night, in the taverns's back rooms
the world's dregs shout
amid clinking bottles
and jingling doubloons.

The genital smell of women
breeds mint flies in the blood,
and sometimes above the din
erupt the crashes of a brawl.

Ay, the buccaneer's Cayona!
Rum and tobacco, fistfights and whores:
pastimes of a ghastly horde
that invokes the devil in twenty tongues.

And when the night—a corsair's flag—
waves unfurled over Tortuga,
the moon, in league with pirates,
stamps its skull against the black.

ᏀᏇ ᏀᏇ ᏀᏇ

Give the buccaneer *boucan* meat,
his long, black-powder musket,
his red shirt, his rawhide sandals,
and his scalding, peppered rum punch.

Canción de Mar

Dadme esa esponja y tendré el mar.
El mar en overol azul
abotonado de islas
y remendado de continentes,
luchando por salir de su agujero,
con los brazos tendidos empujando las costas.

Dadme esa esponja y tendré el mar.
Jornalero del Cosmos
con el torso de músculos brotado
y los sobacos de alga trasudándole yodo,
surcando el campo inmenso con reja de oleaje
para que Dios le siembre estrellas a voleo.

Dadme esa esponja y tendré el mar.
Peón de confianza y hércules de circo
en cuyos hombros luce su acrobático genio
la chiflada y versátil "troupe" de los meteoros . . .

(Ved el tifón oblicuo y amarillo de China,
con su farolería de relámpagos
colgándose a la vela de los juncos.
Allá el monzón, a la indostana,
el pluvioso cabello perfumado de sándalo
y el yatagán del rayo entre los dientes,
arroja sus eléctricas bengalas
contra el lujoso paquebote
que riega por las playas de incienso y cinamomo
la peste anglosajona del turismo.
Sobre su pata única, vertiginosamente,
gira y gira el tornado mordiéndose la cola
en trance de St. Vito hasta caer redondo.
Le sigue el huracán loco del trópico
recién fugado de su celda de islas,
rasgándose con uñas de ráfagas cortantes

Sea Song

Give me that sponge and I'll have the sea.
The sea in blue overalls,
buttoned down with islands
and patched up with continents,
wrestling to escape its basin,
its outstretched arms pushing shores.

Give me that sponge and I'll have the sea.
Farmhand of the Cosmos,
its muscular torso bulging
and its algae armpits secreting iodine,
its plowshare of waves furrowing the endless field
so God may sow it scattering stars.

Give me that sponge and I'll have the sea.
Farm foreman and circus strongman,
on whose shoulders shines the acrobatic genius
of the loony, versatile meteor troupe . . .

(See the slanted, yellow Chinese typhoon,
its festooned lightning lanterns
dangling from the sails of junks.
Over there, as in Hindustan, the monsoon,
its raining hair fragrant with sandalwood
and a scimitar bolt in its teeth,
hurls its electric fireworks at
the opulent pack-boat that spreads,
along incense and cinnamon beaches,
the plague of Anglo-Saxon tourists.
On its one leg the tornado, dizzying,
whirls and whirls biting its tail
in a St. Vitus's dance to its death.
Next the tropic's mad hurricane,
just escaped from its cell of islands
scratching with sharp gust nails

las camisas de fuerza que le ponen las nubes;
y detrás, el ciclón caliente y verde,
y sus desmelenadas mujeres de palmeras
fusiladas al plátano y al coco.

En el final despliegue va el simún africano
—seis milenios de arena faraónica
con su reseco tufo de momia y de pirámide—.
La cellisca despluma sobre el agua
su gigantesca pájara de nieve.
Trombas hermafroditas
con sombrillas de seda y voces de barítono
cascan nueces de trueno en sus gargantas.
Pasa el iceberg, trono al garete,
del roto y desbandado imperio de los hielos
con su gran oso blanco
como un Haakón polar hacia el destierro,
levantado el hocico cual si humease en la noche
la Osa Mayor rodada del ártico dominio;
y mangas de pie alígero y talle encorsetado
ondulan las caderas raudamente
en el salón grisperla del nublado,
y ocultan su embarazo
de barcas destripadas y sorbidas
en guardainfantes pálidos de bruma.)

Dadme esa esponja y tendré el mar.
Minero por las grutas de coral y madrépora
en la cerrada noche del abismo
—Himalaya invertido—
le alumbran vagos peces cuyas linternas sordas
disparan sin ruido en la tiniebla
flashes de agua de fósforo
y ojos desmesurados y fijos de escafandra.
Abajo es el imperio fabuloso:
la sombra de galeones sumergidos
desangrando monedas de oro pálido y viejo;

straightjackets the clouds strap on;
and behind it, the hot, green cyclone
and its tosseled-haired palm-tree wives
barraged with plantains and coconuts.

In the finale blows the African simoon
—six millenia of pharaonic sand's
dessicated smell of pyramid and mummy—.
Above the water, sleet is plucking
its gigantic hen-bird of snow.
Hermaphrodite waterspouts,
with silk umbrellas and baritone voices,
crack thunder nuts with their throats.
From the fractured, jigsaw empire of ice,
drifts the iceberg, rudderless throne
with its great white bear
like a polar, exiled Haakon,
its upward snout seeming to scent in the night
Ursa Major of the arctic dominion;
and in the pearl-gray dance hall of storm clouds
the fleet-footed, corseted typhoons
torrentially undulate their hips
as, under pale, hooped-skirts of fog,
they hide being pregnant
with gutted, waterlogged hulls.)

Give me that sponge and I'll have the sea.
Miner through red and white coral grottos,
in the dead-end night of the abyss
—upsidedown Himalaya—
his way lighted by blurred fish whose mute lamps
silently shoot into darkness
phosphorescent-water flashes
and a diving helmet's fixed, popped eyes.
Below is the empire of fable:
shadows of submerged galeons
bleeding old, washed-out gold coins;

las conchas entreabiertas como párpados
mostrando el ojo ciego y lunar de las perlas;
el pálido fantasma de ciudades hundidas
en el verdor crepuscular del agua . . .
remotas ulalumes de un sueño inenarrable
resbalado de monstruos que fluyen en silencio
por junglas submarinas y floras de trasmundo.

Dadme esa esponja y tendré el mar.
El mar infatigable el mar rebelde
contra su sino de forzado eterno,
para tirar del rischa en que la Aurora
con rostro arrociblanco de luna japonesa
rueda en su sol naciente sobre el agua;
para llenar las odres de las nubes;
para tejer con su salobre vaho
el broderí intangible de las nieblas;
para lanzar sus peces voladores
como últimas palomas mensajeras
a los barcos en viaje sin retorno;
para tragarse—hindú maravilloso—
la espada de Vishnú de la centella,
y para ser el comodín orfebre
cuando los iris, picaflores mágicos,
tiemblan libando en su corola azul,
o cuando Dios como por distraerse,
arrójale pedradas de aerolitos
que él devuelve a las playas convertidas
en estrellas de mar y caracolas.

Dadme esa esponja y tendré el mar.
Hércules prodigioso
tallado a furia de aquilón y rayo
que hincha el tórax en ansia de infinito,
y en gimnástico impulso arrebatado
lucha para salir de su agujero
con los brazos tendidos empujando las costas.

conches half-open like eyelids
showing their blind, moon whites;
the blanched ghosts of cities
sunken in the water's twilight green . . .
remote Ulalumes of indescribable dreams
slimy with monsters that glide without sound
through underwater jungles and afterlife flora.

Give me that sponge and I'll have the sea.
Inexhaustible sea, sea in rebellion
against its fate of laborer eternally forced
to pull the rickshaw that Dawn,
her white-rice face a Japanese moon,
rides over water in her emerging sun;
to fill the wineskins of the clouds;
to knit with brackish stench
the intangible embroidery of fogs;
to send off its flying fish
like the last carrier pigeons
to ships on a voyage of no return;
to swallow—Hindu of marvels—
Vishnu's lightning sword,
and be both gilder and goldsmith
when rainbows, magic hummingbirds,
flutter drinking from their blue corollas,
or when God, as if for fun,
skips against it meteoric stones
that onto beaches it returns recast
as starfish and snail shells.

Give me that sponge and I'll have the sea.
Uncanny Hercules
sculpted with bolts and northerly fury,
that swells its chest to inhale infinity
and, uncontrollable its gymnastic urge,
wrestles to escape its basin,
its outstretched arms pushing shores.

Part IV

1944-1959

Plena de Menéalo

Bochinche de viento y agua . . .
sobre el mar
está la Antilla bailando
—de aquí payá, de ayá pacá—
menéalo, menéalo
en el huracán.

Le chorrea la melaza
bajo su faldón de cañas;
tiemblan en goce rumbero
sus pechos de cocoteros,
y vibrante cotelera,
de aquí payá las caderas
preparan el ponche fiero
de ron con murta y yerbiya
para el gaznate extranjero.
¡Ay, que se quema mi Antilla!
¡Ay mulata, que me muero!
Dale a la popa, chiquilla,
y retiemble tu velero
del mastelero a la quilla
de la quilla al mastelero.

Fija la popa en el rumbo
guachinango de la rumba.
¡Ay, cómo zumba tu zumbo
—huracanada balumba—
cuando vas de tumbo en tumbo,
bomba, candombe, macumba,
si el changó de Mombo-Jumbo
te pone lela y tarumba!
¡Cómo zumba!

Shake It Plena

Rumors between wind and water . . .
On the sea,
the Island is dancing
—back and forth, side to side—
shake it, shake it,
in the hurricane.

Her molasses gushes
under her long sugar-cane skirt;
her coconut breasts
jiggle in rumba joy
as, a cocktail blender,
her whirring hips
mix a stiff rum punch
of mint and myrtle
for foreign gullets.
Ay, my Island's on fire!
Ay, mercy, mulatta!
Swerve your stern, girl,
and shake out your sails
from topmast to keel
from keel to topmast.

Fix your stern on the rumba's
all-this-for-you course.
Ay, how your buzzing zooms
—hurricaned volume—
when bump on bump you move
bomba, candombe, macumba . . .
if the Mumbo-Jumbo Changó
gets you drunk and confused!
How it zooms!

Y, ¡qué rabia! cuando sabia
en fuácata y ten con ten,
te vas de merequetén
y dejas al mundo en babia
embabiado en tu vaivén.
¡Ay, qué rabia!

Llama de ron tu melena.
Babas de miel te acaoban.
Anguila en agua de plena,
pon en juego tus ardites
que te cogen y te roban . . .
¡Cómo joroban tus quites!
¡Ay que sí, cómo joroban!

En el raudo movimiento
se despliega tu faldón
como una vela en el viento;
tus nalgas son el timón
y tu pecho el tajamar;
vamos, velera del mar,
a correr este ciclón,
que de tu diestro marear
depende tu salvación.
¡A bailar!

Dale a la popa el valiente
pase de garbo torero,
que diga al toro extranjero
cuando sus belfos enfile
hacia tu carne caliente:
—Nacarile Nacarile,
Nacarile del Oriente—.

And oh what rage! When wise
in stepping and shaking
your body shimmies and snakes
and leaves the world gaga,
drooling before your swing.
Ay, what rage!

Rum flames your river of hair.
Oozing honey stains you mahogany.
Eel in a water of *plena,*
wiggle for all your worth
lest they net and steal you . . .
How your slickness galls!
Ay, yes, how it galls!

In your rapid whirling
your enormous skirt billows
like a windblown sail;
your thighs are rudders,
your breasts the cutwater;
faster, racing boat of the sea,
to ride out this cyclone,
for your nautical skill
is all that can save you.
Keep dancing!

Swerve your stern boldly
as an exquisite matador,
telling the foreign bull
whose blubber lips crave
your tropical skin:
"Huff, huff all you want,
But you can't have this."

Dale a la popa, danzando,
que te salva ese danzar
del musiú que está velando
al otro lado del mar.
Ondule tu liso vientre
melado en cañaveral;
al bulle-bulle del viento
libre piernas tu palmar;
embalsamen tus ungüentos
azahares de cafetal
y prenda fiero bochinche
en el batey tropical,
invitando al huele-huele
tu axila de tabacal.

Mientras bailes, no hay quien pueda
cambiarte el alma y la sal.
Ni agapitos por aquí,
ni místeres por allá.
Dale a la popa, mulata,
proyecta en la eternidad
ese tumbo de caderas
que es ráfaga de huracán,
y menéalo menéalo,
de aquí payá, de ayá pacá,
menéalo, menéalo,
¡para que rabie el Tío Sam!

Swerve your stern, dancing,
for that dancing saves you
from the Monsieur who ogles you
from across the sea.
Undulate your flat belly
glazed with sugar cane field;
loose your palm tree legs
in the wind's gossiping;
let your ointments perfume
the coffee-field blossoms
as you kindle scorching rumors
around the tropic sugar mills,
inviting to its smelly smell
your tobacco-farm armpits.

While you dance, no power can change
your soul and spunk.
Not Agapitos* from down here,
not "Misters" from up there.
Swerve your stern, mulatta,
steer toward eternity
that gyration of hips
really hurricane gusts,
and shake it, shake it,
this way and that, that way and this,
shake it, shake it,
fanning the rage of Uncle Sam!

*From Agapito's Bar, a 1950s gathering place for statehood advocates.

Bocetos Impresionistas

Vamos, acróbatas modernos,
sobre trapecio de metáforas
a hacer maromas peligrosas
para que el gran público aplauda.
Saco imágenes del bolsillo
como rosas recién cortadas . . .
Heme aquí, de pie en el trapecio,
disparado en mecida larga
hacia la flor que no perfuma,
hacia la estrella que no existe,
hacia el pájaro que no canta.

II

Ese árbol seco
comido de lianas y helechos,
es como el viejo zapatero
siempre enredado entre zapatos
que ahora, de repente, recuerdo . . .
vidas iguales, frías, áridas,
y en torno la llanura
abierta en dilatado bostezo.

III

El buen marido esta mañana
dice a su mujer:—Prepara
las maletas, que voy de viaje—.
Ella lo mira de tal modo
que él comprende, lía un cigarrillo
y lanza una espiral dolorosa de humo.

Impressionist Sketches

Let's climb, modern acrobats,
onto the metaphor trapeze
to perform trecherous stunts
so the great audience applauds.
From my pocket I mine images
like freshly cut roses . . .
Here on the trapeze I stand,
rocking, rocking for my flight
toward the scentless flower,
toward the make-believe star,
toward the bird without song.

II

That hollow tree,
eaten through by lianas and ferns,
resembles the old shoemaker
entangled in dangling pairs,
whom I now suddenly recall . . .
identical lives, cold, dried-up,
and both stand on a plain,
agape in a great yawn.

III

This morning the good husband
said to his wife: "Pack
my bags. I'm taking a trip."
Her eyes answer him so
he gets her point, lights a cigarette,
blows a painful spiral of smoke.

IV

Ni el tranvía, ni el teatro, ni el cabaret pudieron
extirpar la yerba, los árboles y el agua
que aquel hombre llevaba
en la risa, en el chaleco y en la corbata,
y así aquel hombre era
una pradera suelta por las calles.

V

Tierra de hambres y saqueos
y de poetas y azucareros . . .
Antilla perfumada que arrastra
su estómago vacío sobre el agua.
Jaula de loros tropicales
politiqueando entre los árboles.
¡Pobre isla donde yo he nacido!
El yanki, bull-dog negro,
te roe entre sus patas como un hueso.

VI

Tendido boca arriba
me arropo con el cielo
en la noche del trópico
silbante, murmurioso y trompetero.
Tendido boca arriba
en cósmica expansión me voy abriendo
mientras el sueño cierra mis pupilas.
Mas de pronto despierto
con una extraña comezón de mundos,
y miro las estrellas
que como chinches andan por mi cuerpo.

IV

Neither streetcar, theater, nor cabaret
succeeded in uprooting the grass, trees and streams
that man was wearing
in his smile, vest, and necktie,
making of that man
a meadow loose in the streets.

V

Land of hunger and plunder
and poets and sugar bosses . . .
Perfumed isle that drags
its empty stomach over water.
Cage of tropical birds
politicking in the trees.
Poor island of my birth!
The Yankee, a black bulldog,
chews on you, the bone between his paws.

VI

Lying face up,
I blanket myself with sky
at night in the whistler, murmurer,
trumpet-blower tropics.
Lying face up,
I expand to cosmic proportions
as sleep closes my eyes.
But suddenly I awake,
bizarrely itchy with planets,
and see stars crawling
like bedbugs over my body.

VII

En esta hora quieta
de la bahía ancha,
la tarde es puerto sosegado
de penumbra y de calma . . .
La noche entra como un gran navío
y arroja sobre el agua
su primera estrella
como un ancla.

VII

At this quiet hour
before the wide bay,
afternoon is a peaceful port
of penumbra and calm . . .
Night enters like a great vessel
and drops into the water,
like an anchor,
its first star.

Puerta al Tiempo en Tres Voces

I

... Del trasfondo de un sueño la escapada
Filí-Melé. La fluida cabellera
fronda crece, de abejas enjambrada;
el tronco —desnudez cristalizada—
es desnudez en luz tan desnudada
que al mirarlo se mira la mirada.

Frutos hay, y la vena despertada
látele azul y en el azul diluye
su pálida tintura derramada,
por donde todo hacia la muerte fluye
en huida tan lueñe y sosegada
que nada en ella en apariencia huye.

Filí-Melé Filí-Melé, ¿hacia dónde
tú, si no hay tiempo para recogerte
ni espacio donde puedas contenerte?
Filí, la inaprehensible ya atrapada,
Melé, numen y esencia de la muerte.

Y ahora, ¿a qué trasmundo, perseguida
serás, si es que eres? ¿Para qué ribera
huye tu blanca vela distendida
sobre mares oleados de quimera?

II

En sombra de sentido de palabras,
fantasmas de palabra
en el susto que toma a las palabras
cuando con leve, súbita pisada,
las roza el halo del fulgor del alma;

Entrance to Time in Three Voices

I

. . . From the background of a dream, the fleeing
Filí-Melé. Her fluent hair,
sprouts leaves, is hived with bees,
her trunk—nudity crystalized—
is nudity in light so bare,
staring at its bark, you see your stare.

Fruits hang, and her aroused vein
throbs blue and in the blue
her pale bleeding dye dilutes
into the flow all things sail toward death,
in a flight so distant and calm
not one hair of her appears to flee.

Filí-Melé Filí-Melé, toward where
go you, if there's no time to gather you
nor space for you to contain yourself?
Filí, inapprehensible, now trapped,
Melé, numen and essence of death.

And now, to what afterworld must you be
pursued, if indeed you are? Toward what shore
flees your white billowed sail
over chimera-slickened seas?

II

In shades of meanings of words,
phantoms of word;
in the fright that overtakes words
when with light, sudden steps,
the nimbus of the soul's radiance brushes against them;

—rasgo de ala en el agua,
ritmo intentado que no logra acorde,
abortada emoción cohibida de habla—
en el silencio tan cercano al grito
que recorre las noches estrelladas,
y más lo vemos que lo oímos,
y casi le palpamos la sustancia
o en el silencio plano y amarillo
de las desiertas playas,
batiendo el mar en su tambor de arena
salado puño de ola y alga.
¿Qué lenguaje te encuentra, con qué idioma
(ojo inmóvil, voz muda, mano laxa)
podré yo asirte, columbrar tu imagen,
la imagen de tu imagen reflejada
más allá de la música-poesía,
muy atrás de los cantos sin palabras?

Mis palabras, mis sombras de palabras,
a ti, en la punta de sus pies, aupadas.
Mis deseos, mis galgos de deseos;
a ti, ahilados, translúcidos espectros.
Yo, evaporado, diluido, roto,
abierta red en el sinfín sin fondo . . .
Tú, por ninguna parte de la nada,
¡qué escondida, cuán alta!

III

En lo fugaz, en lo que ya no existe
cuando se piensa,
y apenas deja de pensarse
cobra existencia;
en lo que si se nombra se destruye,
catedral de ceniza, árbol de niebla. . .
¿Cómo subir tu rama?
¿Cómo tocar tu puerta?

—stroke of wing in water,
intended rhythm never quite music,
aborted emotion muzzled of speech—
in the silence so close to a scream
it shoots across starry nights
and more than hear we see it
and almost touch its matter;
or in the flat, yellow silence
of deserted beaches
on whose sand drum the ocean pounds
a briny wave-and-seaweed fist.
What idiom finds you, with what language
(glued eye, mute voice, limp hand)
can I capture you, outline your distant image,
the image of your image reflected
far beyond music-poetry,
long before songs without words?

My words, my shadows of words,
reaching up, on tippy toes, toward you.
My desires, my greyhound desires,
emaciated, translucent specters after you.
I, evaporated, diluted, broken,
net stretched over bottomless infinity . . .
You, nowhere in nothingness,
so hidden, so high!

III

In what is fleeting, in what ceases to exist
while being thought,
and the instant no longer thought
exists again;
in what if named is shattered,
cathedral of ashes, tree of mist . . .
How to climb your branch?
How to knock at your door?

Pienso, Filí-Melé, que en el buscarte
ya te estoy encontrando,
y te vuelvo a perder en el oleaje
donde a cincel de espuma te has formado.
Pienso que de tu pena hasta la mía
se tiende un puente de armonioso llanto
tan quebradizo y frágil, que en la sombra
sólo puede el silencio atravesarlo.
Un gesto, una mirada, bastarían
a fallar sus estribos de aire amargo
como al modo de Weber que en la noche
nos da, cisne teutón, su último canto.

Canto final donde la acción frustrada
abre al tiempo una puerta sostenida
en tres voces que esperan tu llegada,
tu llegada aunque sé que eres perdida . . .
Perdida y ya por siempre conquistada,
fiel fugada Filí-Melé abolida.

I believe, Filí-Melé, that in pursuing you
I'm finally finding you,
then I lose you again among seawaves
where you sculpt yourself with a chisel of foam.
I believe that from your sorrow to mine
spans a bridge of musical weeping
so brittle and fragile, that in darkness
only silence can cross it.
One gesture, one glance would suffice
to collapse its abutments of bitter air
in the style of Weber,* Teutonic swan,
who one night gave us his ultimate song.

Final song in which the muzzled action
opens a sharp-noted entrance to time
in three voices that await your arrival;
your arrival though I know you are lost . . .
Lost and at last forever vanquished,
faithful, fleeting, abolished Filí-Melé.

---

*Carl Maria Friedrich von Weber, 19th century German composer of *Euryanthe*
(1823), a wordless opera of gestures.

La Búsqueda Asesina (Poema Inconcluso)

Yo te maté, Filí-Melé: tan leve
tu esencia, tan aérea tu pisada,
que apenas ibas nube ya eras nieve,
apenas ibas nieve ya eras nada.

Cambio de forma en tránsito constante,
habida y transfugada a sueño, a bruma . . .
Agua-luz lagrimándose en diamante,
diamante sollozándose en espuma.

Fugacidad, eternidad . . . ¿quién sabe?
¿Cómo seguir tu alado movimiento?
¿De qué substancia figurar tu clave,
y con qué clave descifrar tu acento?

Yo te maté, Filí-Melé: buscada
a sordos tumbos ciegos, perseguida
con voz sin cauce, con afán sin brida;
allá en agua de sombras resbalada
sobre arena de estrellas encendida;
allá en tumulto de olas espumada
—flor instantánea al aire suspendida—
por la gracia y la luz arrebatada
y en aire sin recuerdo devenida.
De sol a sol, jornada tras jornada,
desde la puesta hasta la amanecida;
tenso afán de tenerte y penetrarte
mi amor ya no fue amor para quererte,
era viento de sangre para ahogarte,
red de oscura pasión para envolverte.

The Killer Pursuit (Inconclusive Poem)

I killed you, Filí-Melé: so buoyant
your essence, so aerial your tread,
almost a cloud already snow,
almost snow already nothing.

Change of form in constant passage,
once been, defected to dream, to mist . . .
Water-light teardropping to diamond,
diamond sobbing itself to foam.

Fleetingness, eternity . . . Who can say?
How to track your winged movement?
From what substance figure your key,
and in what key decode your accent?

I killed you, Filí-Melé: sought
by deaf, blind stumblings, pursued
by unchanneled voice, by intensity unreined;
far off on shadow water sailed
over star-glistening sands inflamed;
far upon tumultous waves foamed
—instant flower in air suspended—
by grace and light abducted
and in air without memory transpired.
Sun to sun, setting to rise,
one day's journey to the next,
tense zeal to possess and penetrate you
my love no longer a love to want you,
but a blood wind to drown you,
a dark-passion net to ensnare you.

¡Oh lirio, oh pan de luz, oh siderado
copo de espuma virgen que con fiero
y súbito ademán hube tronchado!
¿Cómo volverte a tu fulgor primero?

Eras en mí, dentro de mí, presencia
vital de amor que el alma sostenía,
y para mí, fuera de mí, en ausencia,
razón del ser y el existir: poesía.

Y ahora,
silencio, soledad, quietud que añora . . .

¿Qué trompa de huracán hace más ruido
que este calmazo atroz que me rodea
y me tiene sin aire y sin sentido,
sordo de verbo y lóbrego de idea,
y que se anuda a mí con cerco fiero
en yelo ardiente y negro congelado,
cual detrito de acoso y desespero
por mi íntima tensión centrifugado?

Zumbel tú, yo peonza. Vuelva el tiro,
aquel leve tirar sobre el quebranto
que a masa inerte dábale pie y giro
haciéndola cantar en risa y llanto
y en sonrisa y suspiro . . .
¡Vuelva, zumbel, el tiro,
que mientras tires tú me dura el canto!

Oh lily, oh loaf of light, oh starry
virgin foam bough that with a cruel,
impulsive face I would chop down!
How to recover your first radiance?

You, in me, inside me, vital presence
of a love that nourished my soul;
and for me, outside me, in absence,
reason for being and existing: poetry.

And now,
silence, solitude, a yearning peace . . .

What hurricane trumpet blows louder
than this atrocious, orbitting calm
that has me gasping for air and numb,
deaf to words, my thoughts in gloom,
that girds me with a ruthless ring
of hot ice and frozen black,
like a debris of hounding and despair
centrifugally round my inmost force.

You the cord, I a whirling top. Wind up and fling
again over the brokenness, that easy fling
that gave a dead mass spin and balance
making it sing in laughter and tears
and smiles and sighs . . .
Wind up, cord, and fling once more,
for only while you fling my song whirls on!

El Llamado

Me llaman desde allá . . .
larga voz de hoja seca,
mano fugaz de nube
que en el aire de otoño se dispersa.
Por arriba el llamado
tira de mí con tenue hilo de estrella,
abajo, el agua en tránsito,
con sollozo de espuma entre la niebla.
Ha tiempo oigo las voces
y descubro las señas.

Hoy recuerdo: es un día venturoso
de cielo despejado y clara tierra;
golondrinas erráticas
el calmo azul puntean.
Estoy frente a la mar y en lontananza
se va perdiendo el ala de una vela;
va yéndose, esfumándose,
y yo también me voy borrando en ella.
Y cuando al fin retorno
por un leve resquicio de conciencia
¡cuán lejos ya me encuentro de mí mismo!
¡qué mundo más extraño me rodea!

Ahora, dormida junto a mí, reposa
mi amor sobre la hierba.
El seno palpitante
sube y baja tranquilo en la marea
del ímpetu calmado que diluye
espectrales añiles en su ojera.
Miro esa dulce fábrica rendida,
cuerpo de trampa y presa
cuyo ritmo esencial como jugando

The Call

They're calling me from out there . . .
a dry leaf's voice from afar,
fleeting hand of cloud
that disperses in the autumn air.
From above, the call pulls at me
with a star's fragile line;
below, the traveling water's
foam sobbing in fog.
At times I hear the voices,
discover the signs.

Today I remember: a happy day,
the sky cloudless and earth bright;
meandering swallows
stitch the blue calm.
I'm facing the sea as on the horizon
fades the wing of a sailboat;
dissolving, it slowly departs,
and I too disappear inside it.
And when at last I return,
through a thin crevice of consciousness,
how far I find me from myself!
What a strange world surrounds me!

Now, asleep beside me, my love
is resting on the grass.
Her heaving chest
peacefully rises and falls in the ebb
of an urge that, satisfied,
dilutes ghostly indigos under her eyes.
I look upon that warm, exhausted factory,
body both trap and prey,
whose essential rhythm, as if at play,

manufactura la caricia aérea,
el arrullo narcótico y el beso
—víspera ardiente de gozosa queja—
y me digo: Ya todo ha terminado . . .

Mas de pronto, despierta,
y allá en el negro hondón de sus pupilas
que son un despedirse y una ausencia,
algo me invita a su remota margen
y dulcemente, sin querer, me lleva.

Me llaman desde allá . . .
Mi nave aparejada está dispuesta.
A su redor, en grumos de silencio,
sordamente coagula la tiniebla.
Un mar hueco, sin peces,
agua vacía y negra
sin vena de fulgor que la penetre
ni pisada de brisa que la mueva.
Fondo inmóvil de sombra,
límite gris de piedra . . .
¡Oh soledad, que a fuerza de andar sola
se siente de sí misma compañera!

Emisario solícito que vienes
con oculto mensaje hasta mi puerta,
sé lo que te propones
y no me engaña tu misión secreta;
me llaman desde allá,
pero el amor dormido aquí en la hierba
es bello todavía
y un júbilo de sol baña la tierra.
¡Déjeme tu implacable poderío
una hora, un minuto más con ella!

manufactures the aerial caress,
the narcotic cooing, and the kiss
—ardent eve of a pleasure moan—
and I say to myself: I will never have her again . . .

But suddenly she awakes,
and far in the black depths of her eyes,
at once an absence and a departure,
something invites me to its remote shore
and tenderly, without effort, carries me to it.

They're calling me from out there . . .
Ready my rigged vessel waits.
Around it, soundlessly,
darkness curds into gobs of silence.
A hollow, fishless sea,
a vacant, black water
no brilliant vein can penetrate,
no breeze's step ripples.
Motionless shadow floor,
gray terminus of stone . . .
Oh, solitude, alone for so long
it feels like its own companion.

Dutiful agent who brings
a concealed message to my door,
I know why you've come,
so your mission's no secret for me;
they're calling me from out there,
but the love asleep here on the grass
is beautiful still,
and a sun-filled joy bathes the earth.
Grant me, your inexorable power,
one hour, one more minute of her!

Glossary

Agapito   An advocate of statehood for Puerto Rico.

Babbitt   Middle-class American, stereotypical symbol of narrow-mindedness and self-satisfaction. George Babbitt is the protagonist of Sinclair Lewis's 1922 novel Babbitt.

bámbula   Afro-Caribbean dance form.

bayadere   Woman of India.

Boricua   Modifier meaning "Puerto Rican," from the island's original Taíno name, Borikén or Borinquen.

boucan   Originally the French word for barbecue frame, later forming *boucaner,* "to cure meat," evolving to form *boucanier,* "pirate" or "one who cures meat on a barbecue frame" (for which seventeenth-century French pirates were known).

bomba   Afro-Puerto Rican dance form.

cacao   Reddish-brown seed pods used in making chocolate, cocoa, and cocoa butter.

callaloo   Soup prepared in Martinique.

candombe   Caribbean dance originally from an African war dance.

Changó   God of thunder and lightning, highest god in the Afro-Cuban pantheon.

conga	Dance in which dancers form a long line.
Creole	Person of European descent born in the Americas. In Spanish, *criollo.*
Dulcinea	The refined lady whom Don Quixote imagines when looking at the trashy Maritornes.
guanábana	Spiny fruit with a white, tart pulp; soursop.
Haakon	Name of seven kings of Norway.
Kalahari	African desert stretching from South Botswana to East Namibia.
macumba	Caribbean dance form of African origin.
mamey	Fruit with a reddish rind and yellow pulp; mammee apple.
Maritornes	Woman whom Don Quixote believed to be his lady Dulcinea.
Mayombe	Afro-Cuban sect.
mongo	Tribal chief.
Náñigo	Member of a secret Afro-Cuban sect.
Obatalá	Afro-Cuban god.
Papiamento	Dialect of Spanish spoken on the island of Curaçao.
patois	Any language that mixes languages; non-standard speech.
parrot	The word *loro,* or parrot, also formerly signified a black Caribbean islander.
Quimbamba	A faraway, nameless place.
Saladin	Sultan of Egypt and Syria (1138-1193).
Toute chaude	Literally, "all burned."
Tembandumba	A goddess from African legends.
Ulalumes	From Poe's "Ulalume," which Palés interprets as a far-off ideal.
Vishnu	One of the deities worshipped by Hindus.
St. Vitus's Dance	Disturbance of the central nervous system, characterized by involuntary movements of the face and extremities. Also known as chorea.